RightSideUp

Find Your Way
When Military Life
Turns You Upside Down

~

Judy Davis
The Direction Diva

Lindsey!
Here's to living
Right Side Up
Judy Davis

Elva Resa ✳ **Saint Paul**

Right Side Up: Find Your Way When Military Life Turns You Upside Down
© 2014 Judith M. Davis

All personal stories used with permission.

Cover photo © Tim Pannell/Masterfile.
Cover design by Andermax Studios and Connie DeFlorin.

LCCN: 2014029598
ISBN: 978-1-934617-32-8

Printed in United States of America.
10 9 8 7 6 5 4 3 2 1

Elva Resa Publishing
8362 Tamarack Village, Suite 119-106
Saint Paul, MN 55125

www.ElvaResa.com
www.MilitaryFamilyBooks.com

*To my soldier, my hero and
the reason I am a military spouse.
Thank you for believing in me
and loving me unconditionally,
even when I struggle to live right side up.*

*To Heather and Geoffrey (my Alex).
Without your wisdom and honesty
I may never have had the courage
to reach for the stars.*

*To all the incredible military spouses
who continue to encourage me
to make the most of this life.
You inspire me each and every day.*

—jd

Contents

Introduction

The night my whole life changed, I was making dinner when my husband of seventeen years walked through the door. Something was up. He had a look in his eye that meant things were about to change significantly.

Knowing we'd have "the talk" once the kids were settled with homework and we wouldn't be disturbed, we went through the motions of dinner and cleanup. I prepared myself for the worst and hoped for the best. But I was not ready for the news that came out of his mouth: "Babe, I can't do this anymore. The job isn't the same, and I have to leave."

I knew his job as a plant manager in a manufacturing company had become a nightmare since the buyout, but I hadn't expected him to resign! We were barely forty years old, with children a few years away from entering college. We had a home, a life … and nowhere in the world of Judy did "I can't do this anymore" fit with my vision for our future.

I lost it. "What do you mean you can't do this? You've spent years getting where you are now! How will we pay the mortgage or buy food? How will we survive?" I was in full freak-out mode.

He just sat there and let me go, showing no stress, no worry—not what I'd expect from a man making a choice to leave a career and reputation he had worked long and hard to build. Then it dawned on me—I should have known—he had a plan, and it was a big one.

Slowly, I turned, and in the calmest voice I could muster, looking him directly in the eye, I asked, "Geoffrey, if you aren't going to work at Dynamic, what do you want to do?"

I held my breath while he grinned that huge, little-boy "I've got a secret" grin that messes me up every time, and said, "I want to put back on my uniform and serve my country."

I guess I shouldn't have been surprised. He had always been so patriotic. In fact, when we first met, I was impressed that he had served a combination of Army reserves while in high school and active duty after graduation. But by the time we started dating seriously, he was twenty-four and military life seemed to be behind him. I never contemplated being a military spouse.

If you had asked me back then to share my thoughts about what a military spouse does, I could not have told you. At that point, I had only known one military spouse in my life—a cousin I saw only at family reunions, weddings, and funerals. I knew nothing of her life, nor she of mine.

The day my husband put his uniform back on and took his oath, I had no idea what we had signed up for. I just looked at him with pride and soaked in the well wishes from friends and family as we headed into our new adventure.

Our van donned a fresh US Army sticker like a beacon on the back window as we drove across the country to our first duty station. We may as well have written NEWBIES across our foreheads. Like tourists, we stopped to take pictures of the installation entrance. We cheered as we saw the flag flying, and felt nervous showing our crisp new ID cards at the gate. I can only imagine the chuckle enjoyed by the veteran family coming in behind us, watching us gaze with awe at the military vehicles lined up perfectly in a row.

I laugh as I think back to my newbie days: the time I sat outside the housing office and cried like a baby when our housing wasn't available like they said it would be; the hours I spent searching for the grocery store on post, only to find out that it's called a commissary; or the time I misplaced my husband's orders. I could go on and on about my comical blunders in those early years as a military spouse. While it may have taken me way too long to understand that a POA and a power of attorney are the same thing, I have finally come into my own. All those mess-ups got me to where I am today.

We are all newbies at different points along the way. We all have a lot to learn, from acronyms and packing, to deployments and preparing for our final ETS (Expiration of Term of Service).

When I first became a military spouse, I researched online, read books, joined groups, and volunteered. I immersed myself into military culture. I wanted to know what I was getting myself into, and I needed tools and information to help me handle all the new situations coming my way.

I read about the logistics—benefits, leave and earning statements (LES), deployments, and permanent change of station (PCS). But there wasn't a book, website, family readiness group (FRG) leader, or chain of command that prepared me for the emotional roller-coaster ride of military life—the stress, chaos, disrupted home life, and constant change I would now have to manage day in and day out.

I found military life so different from what the media, recruiters, and even my spouse portrayed. I hadn't anticipated the emotional toll.

I knew I couldn't be the only one who found it challenging to survive and thrive as a military spouse. If I was spending my days feeling lost and insecure, other people in the military community were, too.

That's why I wrote *Right Side Up*. Whether you are a newbie, a seasoned spouse, or somewhere in between, my guess is that, at some point, this life has pushed you emotionally.

Each story, page, and exercise in this book comes from

the lessons, mess-ups, and meltdowns I've have over the years. The perspective I share here led me to love military life in a realistic and heartfelt way. I've grown in ways I never knew were possible. You can, too.

Right Side Up addresses some of the unspoken truths that people rarely talk about—the emotional issues we all face as military spouses. I hope that by sharing how I navigated through the storms that blew through our lives, and by offering strategies and perspectives that helped improve my everyday life and emotional well-being, other military spouses—you—can ultimately view each challenging moment as an opportunity.

As you read "A Glimpse of the Life" excerpts, you will see that I get what it's like to feel stressed out and unsure of what's next. I'm here to tell you, it doesn't have to be that way. Each chapter contains proven strategies for overcoming anything military life throws your way.

~

A Glimpse of the Life

I am standing in line outside our post Starbucks early on a Sunday morning. The weather is almost as delicious as my anticipated venti, nonfat, no water, chai (if you haven't had one, you to have try it).

In line are: A lady, obviously straight from the gym, toned arms and all; an Army wife with three kids in tow, just trying to get some caffeine so she can restart her already hectic day (been there, done that); a group of soldiers who, if I had to bet on it, haven't been home since last night and are debating whether or not to pull an all-dayer to go with their all-nighter (so glad those are behind me); the soldier who obviously got stuck with duty this weekend, trying to stay awake for a few more hours until his relief gets in ... and then me—straight from the muddy dog park, after dropping off my husband early for yet another week away in the field—my hair in a ponytail, no makeup, covered in paw prints, and smelling like the gourmet salmon-flavored dog treats that are extra pungent so my puppy pays attention when every other scent is tickling her nostrils (by the way, it doesn't work).

Here we are, all of us and our different lives, in line waiting together. Instantly, we bond over what is the common thread—our Army Strongness. Small conversations start up because we are all here waiting for the doors to open, and we have to pass the time somehow (I wasn't the only one who thought it opened earlier than it does on Sunday).

Beautiful-arm lady is anxiously waiting for her husband to return from a long year in Afghanistan; she can't wait to see him and tell him in person that she reached her goal of losing seventy-five pounds while he was gone. The mom with the kids—her husband left this morning to go back to the sandbox after a much-needed two weeks of R&R, and she's really not sure how she's going to get through the day. The group of party boys, all newbies to the Army, leave for the same place within the week and are, admittedly, a bit frightened. The rest of us have the usual Army life stuff going on, and we are doing our best to find the bright spot in the day.

The amazing thing is that in this line, there is no rank, no judgment, no "my situation is worse than yours," or any "feel sorry for me" attitudes. It's just a group of people who get what each other's lives are like, and in the sharing of our experiences, we end up supporting each other without even trying. Maybe it's the fact that it's so beautiful out, or because it's early on a Sunday. It could even be that we all feel a little raw today, but it's moments like this that make me proud to be in this family, the military family.

Nowhere else can such a diverse group of people come together and form instant bonds. Nowhere else would frightened soldiers help out a frantic mom by holding her baby while she runs after her toddler. Nowhere else but in this line, on this post, and in this family, could a muddy, hair-pulled-up, paw-printed, dog-treat-smellin' spouse, who hadn't had caffeine yet, feel so welcome. The funny thing is that this family changes daily—new faces, new outfits, new situations—but at the root of it all, we have a silent bond that is ours to share no matter where we are, what line we are in, or who we are standing next to.

Yes, it's times like this that I'm proud to be part of this crazy, fun, and unpredictable group of people that have become MY military family.

~

The challenges of this lifestyle can sometimes make you feel like life is turned upside down. I wrote *Right Side Up* as a personal, unique resource for you to use in those moments. I offer ideas and perspective to help you calm the chaos, flush the stress, respond to change, and find your own way.

Use this book. Highlight it, dog ear it, write in it, and reflect on and incorporate the skills and techniques that apply to you. After each chapter, make notes in the back of the book to create your own personalized Right Side Up Plan.

No matter what's going on in your military life, or where you start your day, you'll find in these pages ideas to help you live—and embrace—your military life. Here's to landing right side up!

Chapter 1
Establish a Firm Footing

I believe that being a military spouse is a privilege. Despite all the stress and chaos that can fill my day, being a military spouse is something I am proud of. I do it for my country, my family, and myself. I've wanted to give up and return to civilian life more times than I can count. But instead, I've chosen to change my perspective and embrace military life as best I can. Through it all, I've learned to take better care of myself, build meaningful friendships, and strengthen my family.

Military life is not for the faint of heart. But every challenge, change, and sacrifice is an opportunity to grow into the person you want to be and to experience life in new ways.

The first step in this process is to know who you are and define what being a military spouse means to *you*. This foothold helps you set realistic expectations and encourages you to be flexible, create a great support system, think positively, and become more resilient.

Define Your Role as a Military Spouse

Whenever I watch shows like *Army Wives* or read fiction stories romanticizing the adventures of a military family, I can't help but feel like these stories paint only a partial picture. The notion of the romantic and glamorous side of military life, sprinkled with a bit of heartache for effect, leaves out much of the hard truth, such as the gut-wrenching sobs that escape once we are finally alone after our spouse leaves for a deployment. We don't hear so much about the sleepless nights spent worrying if things will be different when our service member returns home or the times when we just want to throw up our hands and say "I'm done."

The reality is that on any given day, a real military family's life can resemble a scary roller-coaster ride that we are aching to exit—a series of peaks and valleys with a few twists and turns thrown in for excitement. Between the highs and lows, and the fact that change is the only constant, just functioning as a military spouse takes real effort.

When I first started experiencing these feelings, I wondered how anyone could function in this world of constant change and challenges. For a long time, I couldn't. In fact, I spent months feeling about as grounded and insecure as a teenager in the midst of puberty. I struggled with the fact that I no longer knew where I belonged. And then I listened to what a brilliant and seasoned spouse I met had to say. She told me it was time to take a moment out of my crazy schedule to define what *I* wanted my experience as a military spouse to be. She was right.

We can't change how things happen, and we can't anticipate every little glitch or the fact that the military has so much control over our lives. But we can do something. We can define and understand our role, and we can prepare for our own mission. We can create a life where the unexpected becomes our expected. We can choose to know which situations have bigger risks and rewards and prepare ourselves accordingly. We can train, anticipate, and perhaps carry the military spouse equivalent of a gas mask. Despite a lifestyle filled with so many twists, turns, bumps, and changes, with a little preparation we can have a successful mission, reach our ETS date, and enjoy it along the way.

One of the biggest things I discovered was that I couldn't

view my experiences through my civilian filter anymore. Coping skills that worked in the past were no longer effective under the military umbrella. Stress-relieving techniques didn't have the same effect, and boundaries I set were hard to maintain. Each time I entered a new situation, I was starting over. My role had changed, and I had to change with it.

Using information gleaned from defining what I wanted my role to be, I began to create a new filter through which I could experience military life. I began to look for better ways to become involved in my new community. I reached out to develop new relationships with other spouses and stopped isolating myself from my new life. I admitted to those around me that this life was different from what I thought it would be, and I was open and truthful in my shortcomings and need for support.

> Every challenge, change, and sacrifice is an opportunity to grow into the person you want to be and to experience life in new ways.

My newfound transparency was met with understanding, ultimately helping me come to terms with what I needed and wanted from this life. That simple shift took away so much stress, I no longer felt the need to pretend things were going well when they weren't. I could ask, be frustrated, and, most importantly, talk with my family and friends about my struggles. I allowed myself time to adjust to my new role rather than be critical of the fact I didn't have all the answers. By defining my role as a military spouse, I learned to let go of my previous expectations and just let life unfold. My family flourished, and I was able to see the promise of a good life in the months ahead.

I was asked the other day why anyone would *choose* a life with long (and short) separations, constant moves, and lackluster pay, not to mention having to constantly change plans. Love was the first thing that came to mind; love is the reason I supported my husband's desire to return to service in the first place.

But more than once, I asked myself similar questions. What had we done by leaving the comfort of friends, family, and all we had built? Had we really exchanged it all for a life full of unknowns?

The answers initially eluded me, but eventually I found ways to explain our decision and the life I now consider my mission as much as my husband's. I learned to tell people that our family works together to adjust to the frequent changes, and that while it's not always easy, we have come to love and appreciate this lifestyle. I now share that being a military family is not only the hardest thing we have ever done, it's also the most rewarding.

But how did I get here? How did I go from all the questions to finding peace with the answers? It started on the day I accepted the fact that I was a military spouse—the day I rewrote the oath my husband took and tailored it to become a model for my new life.

It wasn't until I wrote it out that I grasped the fact I had accepted the role of a lifetime—a role that only I could decide how to play. I realized that my experience depends on my expectations and my attitude, and, despite all the ups and downs, I am the only one who can control the outcome. I came to understand what this life could be, if I allowed myself to embrace the fact that I was indeed a military spouse.

Military Spouse's Creed

I am a military spouse.

I am a strong member of a special team.

I serve the people of the United States as I support the military values.

I will always be accepting of the mission, even if I don't understand its purpose.

I will never be defeated by deployments, long separations from family/friends, or unexpected challenges.

I will never quit on myself, my service member, or my family.

I will never forget that our mission is bigger than we are.

I am strong physically and mentally. I excel in my role as a military spouse.

I promise to always maintain my home, my children, and myself to the best of my ability.

I am an expert, and I am a professional.

I stand ready to handle anything that comes our way.

I am a guardian of freedom, my home, and the American way of life.

I am a military spouse.

It doesn't matter how long it takes to fully understand your role as a military spouse. The important thing is that you know it is a vital one. Like service members, spouses commit to a greater cause, follow through to the best of our ability, and learn to understand and define ourselves in a supportive way.

Exercise: *Understand Your Perspective*

Think back to the day you became a military spouse. It may have been your wedding day or the day your spouse donned a uniform for the first time. How did you feel? Write down your thoughts. What ran through your mind the first time you sang the national anthem or saw the flag at full staff? What did you imagine life would be like, and what did you hope to experience?

_____

_____

_____

_____

_____

_____

_____

Now think back to the day you *really* became a military spouse. Not the day you got the title, but the day something inside you shifted—the day you accepted the fact that you are part of this military life—good, bad, and ugly.

Reflect on the reality of your life as a military spouse. How does it differ from your initial expectations? Did your initial feelings about military life change once you began living this life day in and day out?

_____

_____

_____

_____

_____

_____

_____

_____

_____

_____

_____

It's important to take the time to think through these reflections and write about your perspective. The way you see, understand, and define your role as a military spouse is the foundation you will build on from this moment forward, and each of us comes to it on our own terms and in our own time. Some embrace being a military spouse, while others choose to bide time until their service is done. Both ways are acceptable if, through the process of reflection, you discover the path that is right for your life.

Exercise: _Define Your Role_

The role of a military spouse is important. We motivate, inspire, support, and take care of the home front, so our service members can do their jobs. We are the foundation upon which the military is built. But until we personally define the way we want to execute our roles, we can never fully embrace all that this lifestyle has to offer. This exercise will help you understand what being a military spouse means to YOU by helping you uncover expectations and define a set of guidelines upon which you can build.

Finish this sentence. A military spouse is:

_____

_____

_____

_____

_____

_____

Now write a job description as if you were applying for this position. Be sure to include all the things you think are or should be your responsibility. For example: A military spouse takes care of children, works outside the home, etc.

As a military spouse, I believe my responsibilities are:

_____

_____

_____

_____

_____

_____

_____

You may think you know the answer to this question, but ask your spouse about his or her expectations of you, or ask your spouse to write a job description of the duties of a military spouse. You may not like what your spouse says, but it's important to understand where he or she is coming from to be able to complete this exercise.

My spouse believes my role is:

_____

_____

_____

_____

_____

_____

What are the major differences between your description and your spouse's? Do you expect more from yourself than your spouse does or vice versa?

_____

_____

_____

_____

_____

Based on what you have written down so far, when thinking of your role (as defined by you and your spouse) how do you feel? Overwhelmed? Proud? Stressed? Accomplished?

_____

_____

_____

If you could start all over again, what would be your ideal role as a military spouse? What do you wish your daily life looked like today? What are the things you want to do? What feels fulfilling to you?

_____

_____

_____

_____

How is the ideal role you just defined different from the way you function now? List out the differences in the role you play now verses your ideal role.

_____

_____

_____

_____

_____

Ask yourself what needs to change so you can move closer to your ideal and feel good about the role you play in your family's overall mission. What can you do differently? How can you impact your family, your community, and your life while still holding true to what is important to YOU? List a few actions or situations you can change immediately to make your life better and move you closer to your ideal role as a military spouse.

_____

_____

_____

_____

_____

_____

_____

Become Mission Ready

If there is one thing I have learned from my time as a military spouse, it is that if I am not together physically and emotionally, I'm not happy and life stinks. On and off during those first months as a military spouse, I wondered if I would ever learn to embrace my new role. Then I heard this saying: "A prepared spouse is a happy spouse. And a happy spouse is always a good thing!"

That saying carried an underlying message (preparation leads to happiness) that became vital to me in the weeks to follow. It opened my eyes to the idea that it was possible to be a military spouse *and* find joy at the same time.

I won't pretend I have the secret to lifelong happiness, because I know happiness looks different for each of us. But I do know that we all can find happiness and joy in this military life, by preparing and empowering ourselves.

One of my passions is to help others. As a civilian, I was happiest when speaking to a room full of aspiring business owners. I loved sharing my struggles, triumphs, and experiences in a way that could help make someone else's journey just a little bit easier. That passion didn't change when we became a military family.

What did change was my perceived ability to continue to do something so important to me amidst all the unique demands that were new to my life. I tried everything from working longer hours to juggling schedules, but I quickly became exhausted and burned out. I learned that I needed to take care of my own basic needs first.

When we take care of our basic needs, we generate enough strength, energy, and resilience to carry us through the most difficult times and also have energy to follow our passions.

Yes, taking care of ourselves is easier to say than do, especially with kids running around, dinner to be made, or a spouse deployed to some "exotic" place like Afghanistan. It can feel like just one more thing to do. But the result—calmer days, less stress, and more happiness—is worth the effort.

Military spouses need more than food, shelter, money, and water to survive. We need things that will keep us grounded, balanced, and supported in the roles we have defined for ourselves. Most of all, we need:

- Flexibility
- Support
- A healthy mind-set
- Resilience

Stretch Your Flexibility

The comfort of routines (especially when our service member is away) helps us feel more in control of our life. But control doesn't necessarily equate to happiness. In fact, too much control can leave a person feeling drained, disappointed, and unhappy.

In the military, situations change often. That's the every day reality. The sooner I learned to accept that fact, the more flexible I became, and eventually our entire family's daily life became easier.

If you aren't naturally a wing it type of person, learning to be more flexible takes practice. Just as stretching your muscles makes them more flexible, stretching your perspective and adapting your responses goes a long way in helping you become more flexible.

When I first became a military spouse, I naively believed that if I were organized enough or prepared enough, nothing could throw me off. I thought I could control the military beast. That mind-set brought with it a lot of unnecessary stress until I learned that, while I can't control what the military demands, I can find ways to roll with the changes rather than go on a rant or become derailed. I can adjust to the system rather than fight it.

Responding to change is an aspect of military life I'm still fine tuning, but I've come a long way since the days when a last-minute call would completely ruin my week. I learned that better communication and the simple act of setting boundaries can make all the difference in the world.

By letting my family and friends know what I was (and wasn't) willing to be flexible about in the parts of our lives we did have control over, I created an environment where I didn't have to fight for what I needed. My husband learned which situations required him to put our family first, and now, I no longer get frustrated when we need to adjust our lives because of his commitment to his job and military unit.

Early on, when I had one of my bubble-burst meltdowns after learning of a last-minute field training event that con-flicted with school confer-ences, a seasoned Army wife reminded me that no date, no homecoming, no mission, no training was ever "a go" until it happened. Not only did that advice help me on that day, I can't tell you how many times that tidbit of brilliance has saved me from sleepless nights and hurt feelings.

> *Countless hours of stress and frustration have been avoided because I became flexible and adopted the simple mind-set that "it's not a go until it goes."*

Countless hours of stress and frustration have been avoid-ed because I became flexible and adopted the simple mind-set that "it's not a go until it goes." Sure, I sometimes scramble when a time is pushed up, but rarely am I disappointed when plans are delayed. It's about acknowledging and accepting that I'm not in control and finding coping strategies to be okay with that. It's about attitude and flexibility.

Exercise: *Adapt to Change*

What are you good at adjusting to when asked to do so? Think of a few recent examples when you considered yourself flexible and adaptive.

_____

_____

_____

_____

_____

_____

_____

Describe a recent challenge when you felt you should not have had to be flexible. How did this make you feel?

_____

_____

_____

_____

Do you have routines or schedules that limit your ability to be flexible? What other reasons make it difficult for you to wing it or adapt to change?

_____

_____

_____

_____

_____

_____

_____

List ideas you can try, such as setting boundaries and effectively communicating your own needs, that will help limit upheaval in aspects of your life you have more say in.

_____

_____

_____

_____

_____

_____

Brainstorm ways you can create space to be more understanding and open to last-minute changes.

_____

_____

_____

_____

_____

_____

_____

Secure Your Support

One of the great things about being part of the military community is that support isn't far away and it covers a wide variety of life topics. From newcomer orientation to end of service veterans benefits, behavioral health to suicide prevention, budgeting to parenting tips, there are support resources for everyone. Books, organizations, and services, both online and otherwise, are available to meet your specific needs.

The best thing you can do for yourself is spend time exploring what is available to you *before* you need it.

There is no one-size-fits-all personal support system. It's up to you to find one that fits your lifestyle. Some people prefer to lean on family and close friends, while others access resources online or use those available on an installation. Whatever you choose, having a system in place will reduce your personal stress level and allow you to relax and enjoy new experiences.

It took me a while to discover my preferred method of finding and getting the support I need. What helps me most is having a small group of close battle buddies. Our service members have battle buddies, why shouldn't we?

The type of support battle buddies provide has saved my sanity more than any other resource and has become my go-to strategy when life gets crazy. My battle buddies and I rely on each other without requiring an excessive amount of time and energy, and knowing I can ask any one of these women to be at my side on a moment's notice gives me comfort.

> The type of support battle buddies provide has saved my sanity more than any other resource and has become my go-to strategy when life gets crazy.

My battle buddies provide comic relief and kick my butt when I need an attitude adjustment. They "ride the ride" with me, hold my hand as I slowly make my way up that big hill, scream with me as I rush down the other side, and laugh with me for peeing my pants while doing it. This is the kind of support I need to thrive as a military spouse.

Everyone's needs are different. No matter what works for you, I encourage you to give the battle buddy strategy a try. Reach out and connect with someone you trust.

<u>Exercise:</u> *Set Up Your Personal Support System*

Identify five people you can count on to be there for you in times of struggle or crisis.

Name   Phone/Email

_____

_____

_____

_____

_____

Compose a potential battle buddy list. Your battle buddies might be the same or different people from the above support. It takes time to find a battle buddy who truly supports you in a positive way. Take your time and focus on your needs, especially related to military life, and whether or not the person will be there for you when you really need it. Next to the person's name, include notes about how this person positively supports you or concerns you have about this person being your battle buddy.

Battle Buddy   Support or Concerns

_____

_____

_____

_____

_____

   List five websites or blogs that provide tips and information to make your life easier. Ask a friend for suggestions if
you cannot identify five on your own.

_____

_____

_____

_____

_____

   List five other resources you can use for support in times
of crisis or when you need new information or perspective.

_____

_____

_____

_____

_____

Think Healthy Mind-set

I have always believed that attitude and outlook directly affect happiness. Military life is hard enough without making it worse with a veil of negativity, jealousy, or a victim attitude. Wouldn't you agree?

In those early years, my thoughts had a tendency to become my own worst enemy, especially when my spouse was deployed or away on an assignment. I worried all the time. I misconstrued innocent comments and wasted hours rehashing a long-over event.

Eventually, I learned to shift my thoughts and focus on the good things going on in my life. I made a conscious effort to replace each negative thought with a positive one. If I found myself judging the way a fellow spouse handled a situation, I immediately replaced that thought with something the person did right. Rather than feel frustrated by the "hurry up and wait" mentality at many of the offices on post, I began to carry a bag full of items and tasks to productively pass the time. By not judging or questioning, I became able to focus on thoughts that help me improve and enjoy my life. Slowly, one moment at a time, I shifted my mind-set, and I began living right side up.

One thing that helped me with this shift is what I call the "Stop the Twirl" technique. Whenever I find myself and my thoughts beginning to twirl, I say "stop" and immediately focus on something positive. For example, if I begin down the "Is he safe?" road, my mind wants to think about all that could go wrong on my husband's mission. In order to stop the twirl, I say "STOP" out loud and immediately begin to think about his safe homecoming. I brainstorm the menu, the clothes, how I will decorate the house, etc. This shift takes my mind off the negative and places it on something positive.

This technique works well for that occasional twirly thought pattern; however, if you have been getting frustrated, obsessing over the same issues, or experiencing anxiety or the blues on a regular basis, you may need something more. If your twirl is affecting your ability to function in your daily life, please seek professional help.

Exercise: *Stop the Twirl*

What makes you feel in a twirl?

_____

_____

_____

_____

_____

_____

_____

What are the things you tend to ruminate about?

_____

_____

_____

_____

_____

_____

What are some ways you can use this "stop" technique to take your mind off the negative and focus on the positive?

_____

_____

_____

_____

_____

_____

Practice Resilience

All throughout the military community, we hear about resilience—the ability to recover from or adjust to change. We are told how important it is to have the skills to be able to bounce back and become strong and healthy again after something bad or stressful happens.

Had I really paid attention and listened to those resiliency briefings, I would not have found myself in the hospital the week my husband returned from his last deployment. Trust me, recovering from heart issues in room 304 is not the way to celebrate a spouse's homecoming.

~

A Glimpse of the Life

Looking back, I can see that our homecoming was ruined not because of my health crisis, but because I hadn't made myself a priority while he was gone. I didn't have the energy or stamina to be resilient.

During the deployment, I was like every other spouse in our unit: tired, emotionally drained, stressed out, and sexually deprived (hey, just being honest). I was ready for this rotation to be over. But instead of taking care of myself, I kept pushing, dismissing the signals, and ignoring the hints to slow down. Then one day, whammy! No more subtle reminders; instead, there was an ambulance ride to the nearest hospital bed.

Following my health scare, I was able to get back on track by quitting everything I was involved in and slowly adding back the activities and social life that didn't drain or stress me out. Before I left the hospital, I resigned from every activity, car pool, and volunteer position. I took a hiatus from my work and allowed myself time to heal and be. I looked to my closest friends to pick up the slack and help me get my kids to the activities they loved. I cut back on our busy schedules so we could spend more time together as a family at home. I found that the less I had on my plate, the more resilient I could be.

~

To be a resilient military spouse, you don't have to pretend that everything is under control or that you can handle things easily when faced with a crisis. Instead, be realistic about what is going on, reach out for support, and be open to learning new coping skills. Each of these strategies will ensure you grow stronger from the experience.

Resilience is learned over time. At the core of every resilient spouse is a desire to prepare for the worst and hope for the best. How do you prepare yourself for the unexpected and not let it land you in the hospital when homecoming is the only thing on your mind? You begin by making sure you are healthy and strong both physically and emotionally before a challenge arises.

Taking care of yourself is a building block to true resilience and it is something that looks different for each person. Maybe you need to start the process by eliminating everything, like I did. Or perhaps you'll add crafts or coffee with a friend. Heck, taking a nap may be just what you need. No matter what it is, when you take care of yourself, you have the energy to deal with unexpected challenges that come up. Resilience will follow.

<u>Exercise:</u> *Recharge Your Energy Source*

What do you currently do on a regular basis to take care of yourself? How do you recharge your energy, release your stress, or relax your mind?

_____

_____

_____

_____

_____

Make a list of things that make you feel good and help you recharge, regroup, and de-stress.

_____

_____

_____

_____

From your list, select an activity you are willing and able to do to take better care of your own needs.

Daily:

_____

Weekly:

_____

Monthly:

_____

Throughout this book, with each exercise, reflection and story, you are learning and enhancing different skills to become more resilient.

What particular aspect of your physical or emotional health do you most hope to strengthen or pay attention to over the next few weeks?

_____

_____

_____

_____

What actions can you take to support yourself?

_____

_____

_____

Create Your Own Right Side Up Plan

Sometimes when we are in the middle of a situation, it can be hard to remember how to use what we've learned. It takes practice—and sometimes a cheat sheet that you can refer to when life gets crazy.

Turn to the "In the Moment: Your Right Side Up Plan" on page 131. Gather your thoughts about the information and ideas from this chapter.

Reflect on how you can apply these ideas, along with your own strategies, to create a personalized Right Side Up Plan for your life.

Chapter 2
Calm the Chaos

With frequent moves, job changes, long distance communication, and all the other demands of military life, it's easy to get sucked into the whirling vortex of chaos. Add to that a natural pull during deployment to fill the void with busyness (if I'm always busy, I won't notice he is gone), watch more TV, and speak in an outdoor voice to drown out the quiet, and everything gets kicked up a notch.

When you get caught up in the spinning vortex, it's easy to let your coping skills fall by the wayside, forget to take care of yourself, make judgments based on feelings rather than facts, focus on challenges rather than blessings, lose patience, quit seeing the good in people, and have an increased need to be heard. You may even begin to resent your role as a military spouse. I've been there.

The vortex used to be such a big part of my military life, it seemed like part of the benefit package I received with my ID card. But once I recognized it as a force that did not serve me well, I no longer felt trapped by it. When intensity crept in, I turned down the volume.

Learning to acknowledge what was going on helped me discover that the loudness of everything around me was actually a cover-up. The chaos, along with my need to keep busy, were indications I wasn't dealing with something going on in my life.

So what can you do when life is a chaotic mess and you feel the magnetic pull of the vortex? I have discovered five

strategies that help me calm the chaos in my life:
- Get quiet
- Create a no-drama zone
- Manage reactions
- Feel empowered
- Guide end-of-day thoughts

Get Quiet

The first key to calming the chaos of military life lies in the ability to allow quiet into your world when life is anything but quiet.

When the volume of my world increases, I turn down the TV, drive in silence, or step outside to get some fresh air. If it's bad enough, I've even been known to shut off my phone.

Why is this strategy so important? Because in the quiet, you find solutions for dealing with whatever is going on. In the quiet, you are able to catch your breath again. You find your true power and strength. Quiet lets your mind deal with the stress and disorder of military life.

Quiet can be found anywhere—in an airport, a waiting room at the pediatrician's office, even in a car with screaming teenagers!

Think back to your best vacations, and ask yourself what they have in common. My best and most rewarding getaways were those filled with quiet moments spent recharging my battery and getting back to the basics. The lazy beach strolls, the swoosh of skis down the mountain, the sound of the tide coming in, or the peace that fell over the cabin once the kids were finally asleep.

With a bit of practice you will see that, no matter where you are, who you are with, or how insane the environment is, you have the ability to check out and get quiet, even if it's only for a couple of seconds.

A few years ago, I had the pleasure of meeting Beth Beulow, The Introvert Entrepreneur. Beth says, "When we're in a highly stimulating, bustling environment, it can be challenging to maintain a sense of inner calm. Introverts are especially sensitive to this. We can feel our energy being pulled right out of our bodies by all of the activity around us."

I'm not an introvert by nature, but when military life gets insane or I'm at an FRG meeting days before deployment, I can quickly relate to what Beth is saying. At those times, I use Beth's Get Quiet Techniques to find calm anywhere and everywhere (adapted with her permission).

Get Quiet Technique #1: Shake & Stretch

Dogs do certain things to calm themselves down when surrounded by stress. Take a cue from your dog and practice calming behaviors: Yawn, shake your head and hands, and do a good full body stretch (on your tippy toes, hands in the air). This exercise helps release anxiety and reconnect you to your body, helping you feel grounded and centered instantly.

Get Quiet Technique #2: Observe

Adopt the attitude of an observer. The act of observing rather than interacting helps you detach a bit from the activity and chaos going on around you. By releasing yourself from the expectation you have to do *anything* (for instance, talk to someone, help in the kitchen, be especially witty or charming), you give yourself a little breathing room. By watching the group interact, you can gather information and choose more thoughtfully where it makes sense for you to step in and move from observer to participant.

Approaching situations as an observer gives me at least the illusion of control, which contributes greatly to my ability to remain calm.

Create a No-Drama Zone

You know the type. You may even have a tendency to be one of them: that spouse who thrives on drama and goes out of the way to uncover all the yuckiness associated with military life. You say it's a beautiful day and *wham*, the drama spouse is talking about the lady who had the nerve to walk out of her house with *that* on. You share a challenge you are struggling with, and the drama spouse comes back with a story about how he or she had it worse. Yes, drama spouses are a force to be reckoned with.

Drama is an effective distraction from the laundry, the kids, the job, or whatever task needs to be handled at that moment. But participating in drama is a surefire way to do the exact opposite of calming the chaos in your life. How do I know this? Because I lived it at our first duty station.

~

A Glimpse of the Life

When we first came back into the Army, we weren't the normal military family. Our kids were in high school; we had been married for several years; and other than my husband, who originally got out before we were married, no one in our family had military life experience. Everything was different, and I had no idea how to function in this new system. We all just wanted to fit in.

Fast forward a few months to a BBQ we were hosting for my husband's soldiers and their families. I looked around, and it was drama spouse city. It seemed like every conversation was full of complaints about military life. Spouses were complaining about training schedules and an upcoming deployment. Soldiers were complaining about fatigue, finances, and various other issues. And we, the Davis family, were fitting in perfectly.

No wonder our adjustment from corporate America to the military lifestyle was so difficult! We had not only surrounded ourselves with the energy-sucking drama spouses, we were on the verge of becoming just like them—and that was NOT okay!

Shortly after that eye-opening BBQ, things changed. We sought out people who believe, like we do, that serving in the military is a privilege. We got involved in the activities and events that highlighted what the Army does right. Eventually, the drama spouses disappeared.

Sure, for a time it was a bit lonely, but we learned an important lesson that year. We learned that the right friendships are available at each and every duty station; it just takes some time to find them.

~

The BBQ experience made me see how easy it is to get caught up in a cycle of negativity without even knowing it. It also taught me that, if I'm not careful, I can end up being part of something that's not in my best interest. Like many other newbie military spouses, I was afraid of what I didn't know, and I was eager to connect with anyone.

At a time when every aspect of military life seemed overwhelming, chaotic, and challenging, it was natural to seek out someone who understood. I needed a fellow spouse who got military life and got me. I was easily swept up by the people who pointed out the negative side of military life because I was thrilled to have someone to share my woes with. I was glad I wasn't greeted with the "you signed up for it" response I received from my civilian friends.

But after a while, it felt more like I was caught in the crosshairs of a drama spouse eager for any ear. The drama spouse who targeted me wasn't interested in actually helping me move through my challenges or learn the ropes of military spouse living. She was looking for someone to commiserate with. We got together for coffee and complained about our spouses' schedules, the unfair demands on their time, and the fact that no one understood how hard this life is. I spent weeks wishing for my old life back.

Then one day, I realized that whenever I spent time with this drama spouse, I felt horrible. Instead of actually helping me adjust, the drama spouse was adding fuel to the fire. The more I tried to find solutions and resources that moved me forward, the more she belittled my actions. I tried to share the strategies I was learning and how I was beginning to see opportunities within the military community. Eventually, my drama spouse moved on when I chose not to participate in the negativity anymore. And I'm better off for it.

When you choose to be a drama spouse or hang out with or even listen to one, the benefit of that conversation, that diversion, that fleeting moment of connection evaporates. Over time, drama wears out everyone involved and affects reputations and perceptions of character and integrity.

As a new military spouse, I felt trapped by the drama, until I realized I had a choice. Instead of sitting idly by as someone dished dirt on a fellow spouse, I chose to step away or divert the conversation to something more positive. Rather than spend time playing the "who's got it worse" game, I chose to empathize with other spouses and offer real solutions and encouragement.

As I began acting from this perspective, an interesting thing happened. The conversations around me shifted, and the drama decreased. My decision to end my participation created a ripple effect in the lives of those around me.

So how do you know when you are actively participating in the drama? Sure, it's easy to recognize when someone else is gossipy and out of line, but seeing it in yourself isn't always as straightforward. The conversation you have with your neighbor about the girl down the street, the snide remark about someone's outfit or behavior, listening in when another spouse belittles someone else, all seem innocent enough, but these behaviors are the foreplay to full-blown drama.

A good rule of thumb, which helps me determine if I am going down the drama road, is to THINK and ask myself the following questions. (Various forms of this acronym have appeared in stories and poems dating back to 1835 to guide actions that benefit everyone.) If I can't answer yes to each of the following, it is a sure sign it's best not to open my mouth or participate at all.

T	Is it TRUE?
H	Is it HELPFUL?
I	Is it INSPIRING?
N	Is it NECESSARY?
K	Is it KIND?

Participating in drama will take you off course and away from the calm life you are working so hard to create. Identify the drama spouses in your life, and choose to change how you interact with them.

Exercise: *Ditch the Drama*

Each of us has dramatic times in our lives, but how we choose to handle them determines whether or not the drama prevents us from living a calm, peaceful life. These questions will help you better understand how you respond when life hands you lemons, so you can learn from it, change future behaviors, and limit the drama in your life.

Describe a stressful situation for you (current or past).

_____

_____

_____

_____

When you first learned about this situation, what was the first thing you did? Did you call someone to complain, cause a scene, take a moment to assess what was going on?

_____

_____

_____

Did your first action move you toward resolution, or did it add to the chaos? Why?

_____

_____

_____

What would have been a more effective action to take?

_____

_____

_____

Manage Reactions

It doesn't matter if it's a last-minute change in flight times, postponed orders, or a misplaced travel voucher, the way I react makes all the difference in the world. I'm the one my family turns to for cues, guidance, and strength whenever something occurs. If I am calm, our world is calm; but if I respond in a "mom has lost it" type of way, chaos and mayhem are sure to follow.

On the good side, the ability to react quickly to a variety of situations helps me keep our home running smoothly. This skill helps me juggle the multitude of demands placed on our time and our life, and allows me to shift easily from "Mom, I'm hungry" or "Where is my ruck sack?" to helping a fellow spouse in crisis without skipping a beat.

On the other hand, reacting to sudden stressors can also create an instant avalanche of emotions that pushes me to take action that's not very conducive to a peaceful life.

Think about the last time you truly lost it. Perhaps what someone said or the way they responded triggered an instant feeling that ran like hot lava through your veins. The next thing you knew, you were reacting like a crazy person without even thinking about it.

Been there, done that. Those uncontrollable reactions create the chaos and stress that put me into what I call a tornado of intensity. When that happens, it feels like everything is a priority, nothing gets done, and I run around like a chicken with its head cut off in the middle of a frozen pond.

~

A Glimpse of the Life

One of my challenges when I first became a military spouse was that my husband wasn't around much. I got so angry when I had to make decisions that affected all of us but couldn't reach him for his input. Eventually, I made the mistake many military spouses make: I quit worrying about his opinion. It made my life easier. I stopped asking and listening because, in my head, he wasn't around anyway, so what did it matter, right? BIG MISTAKE!

This reaction wasn't healthy or productive. The lines of communication in our marriage deteriorated quickly, leaving us both feeling angry and blaming each other for our frustration. I felt like I was being treated like a child and had to ask permission to make a decision, and he felt like I didn't care what he thought anymore. We were both partially correct.

The real problem was that we had quit doing the most important things in a relationship: listening and respecting each other's feelings. Instead of interacting with each other, we were reacting to the situation, and the result was disastrous.

Thankfully, we got back on track and came up with a plan that worked for both of us. I explained the frustration I felt when I had a timeline in which I needed to make a decision and couldn't reach him, and he shared how he didn't like me making decisions that would impact his life without consulting him first.

By talking it out, we came up with a solution that gave me the flexibility I needed on many issues and a clear understanding of what types of things he needed me to include him in before I committed for both of us. Now, neither of us assumes we know what the other person thinks, and we are both much happier.

~

Military life is so full, everything seems like a priority that needs an immediate response. You might think, as I did, that reacting quickly will prevent your life from entering into a free fall. But spending too much time reacting and not enough time interacting with the people, places, and things around you, causes more pain than peace.

When you pay attention to how you respond to a situation, you can identify and understand the things that push your buttons. You can eventually defuse the triggers and interact in a calmer, more effective way.

Up until a few years ago, I never really understood that my tipping point almost always stemmed from an emotional place rather than a physical one. I came to realize that my reactions, not the actual situations themselves, were responsible for causing my life to spiral out of control in the first place. When I began to recognize that certain thoughts, situations, and people triggered a bigger emotional response from me, I eventually began to see where MY actions (a.k.a. reactions) needed to change.

An interesting thing happened when I learned to interact with a situation rather than react to it. I immediately began to see change. Instead of assuming I knew why the other person did what they did, I asked questions. Instead of jumping to a conclusion with limited information, I researched. Instead of placing judgment or blame, I listened.

> I came to realize that my reactions, not the actual situations themselves, were responsible for causing my life to spiral out of control in the first place.

These little changes in my behavior made a huge difference. Interacting to things rather than reacting to them brought a new sense of calm and balance to my life.

Exercise: *Understand Your Reactions*

This exercise is designed to help you think through and identify the people, places, and situations that cause you to react rather than interact.

Describe a situation in your life that triggered a domino effect of negativity. Who was involved? Where did it happen?

_____

_____

_____

_____

_____

How did you respond?

_____

_____

_____

Exercise: *See Patterns Emerge*

As you continue to understand how you react, you will uncover repeating patterns in your life. Once you recognize how you behave, you can put coping strategies in place to help you. Use this exercise whenever you find yourself reacting in a way that causes stress and anxiety. Over time, it will help you focus on areas to work on.

As you answer the questions, think about your feelings, the people involved, and any similarities in situations, locations, or other details. Consider patterns in your behavior or the behavior of others that cause you to react and reinforce negative cycles.

How do you behave when you react?

_____

_____

_____

How do you behave differently when you interact?

_____

_____

_____

What situations cause you to react rather than interact?

_____

_____

_____

Are there certain people or places that trigger a reaction?

_____

_____

_____

What situations trigger you over and over?

Situation #1:

_____

_____

What can you do to improve the situation?

_____

_____

_____

Situation #2:

_____

_____

What can you do to improve the situation?

_____

_____

_____

Situation #3:

_____

_____

What can you do to improve the situation?

_____

_____

_____

Feel Empowered

"Don't they get that you have a family?"

"But we have plans."

"What do you mean they won't let you come home for Thanksgiving?"

Early on in my life as a military spouse, I was naive enough to think that questions like these were unique and helpful. I thought they deserved the attention of the powers that be, and I was often frustrated that the answers I needed were not readily given to me.

The fact that our lives belonged to that funky hat-wearing guy they call Uncle Sam just didn't fly in my world. I fought it, got frustrated, and was pretty pissed off every time our schedule had to be rearranged because duty called and someone or something needed my husband's immediate attention. I found myself feeling like an injured victim with no control over my situation or my life.

From arguments with my husband to frustration with my kids, our first few months in the military were full of tears and regret, and I actually found myself hating my life for the first time ever. Little did I know, my feelings and the ensuing chaos were due to the fact I spent most of my time fighting with the reality of military life.

I am pretty sure I wasn't the first military spouse who was told by a significant other that I really needed to understand that certain things just go with the territory. It took me a while to realize that our time and a big portion of our lives were no longer our own.

Military life can be unfair, and families often take the brunt of it. It's up to us to dig out our best lemonade recipe when we get handed some nasty lemons.

But here is the cool thing. As soon as I stopped feeling sorry for myself and began to understand that there were ways to shift my mind-set about military protocol and the things I couldn't control, the chaos and stress melted away. Don't get me wrong; sometimes I still throw a pretty good fit when our life gets turned upside-down because someone up the chain makes a unilateral decision that affects my family. But for the most part, it's not an issue that lingers for very long. I see it as part of our life, and I'm good with that.

What changed? And how did things shift? The difference in how my life feels now is that I no longer act like a victim or stew in the anger. Instead of commiserating with another spouse, I seek out solutions and let go of the things that don't serve me well.

~

A Glimpse of the Life

Recently, lost paperwork and a young soldier who didn't understand the impact his actions would have on someone else's career prevented my husband from attending a course he needed for promotion eligibility. To make matters worse, my husband was successfully working a position two pay grades above his own and this promotion was important. Our family suffered through longer work hours. My husband dealt with added stress and responsibility. There were no pay increases or incentives to speak of and I was furious.

I didn't understand how my husband was able to see this as a temporary glitch and that the situation would work itself out. I couldn't get past the impact on our lives and the unfairness of the situation. It wasn't until he pointed out that this added responsibility would become a plus in his career trajectory that I saw the flaw in my thinking.

Instead of looking for the positive, I was focused on the negative impact the situation had on my daily life and on finding someone else to blame for it. Instead of admitting that in the long run the benefits would far outweigh the challenges, I allowed a victim mentality to take over. Even though I know the difference between an empowered spouse's mind-set and a victim spouse's mind-set, the thought process I had adopted left me knee deep in the yuck of it all.

This realization helped me see that, instead of supporting my husband through a difficult time, I was actually making things worse for him. So I looked inside myself and realized that my behavior and attitude were not in alignment with the empowered spouse mind-set I know helps me deal with this life in a healthy, proactive way.

By accepting that the situation was out of my control, I adjusted my thoughts and stopped making things worse. I quit feeling victimized and began to take action to make the situation better. I made time in my schedule to bring my husband lunch and hang out for a few minutes in the middle of the day. I supported him in making the most of an unfair situation by picking up the slack at home, so he could spend time with the kids.

The result came in small victories. We learned new ways to show that we both knew we were a priority for the other. Our family time was more focused, and my husband developed a new respect for how I handled it all. The mind-set of empowerment helped me be there for my husband in a way that acting like a victim never could.

~

It takes focused effort to stay out of victim-ville because it's easy to get roped into the "who has it worse" game. I can't tell you how many times I've seen a spouse share a challenge only to be outdone by another.

Do not compare your situation to others'. No matter how similar your lives are, you don't know what the other person may be going through. It's natural to feel as though you have earned an occasional visit to victim-ville, but it is important to do whatever you can to squash the thoughts that hold you back, and replace them with actions that move you forward.

It's about being grateful when things go right ... and not focusing on the struggles.

For me, the best way to do that is to seek out positive people, places, and things. It's about being grateful when things go right and work in my favor, and not focusing on the struggles or times when things don't turn out as I had hoped. When danger and heartache are prevalent, this isn't an easy thing to do; it requires effort and awareness but, when done, pays off exponentially.

From my experience, there isn't a chain of command out there that wants to disrupt your life any more than they want to disrupt their own. There are reasons things are done, and more often than not, you will never know those reasons. It's the military and, you guessed it, it goes with the territory. While it may not seem fair, you do have a choice. You can accept the situation. You can take action to facilitate change.

What won't help is to whine, gripe, and complain about your life and the challenges that come up.

People who view themselves as victims never find real happiness or calm the chaos in their lives. The best way to avoid feeling victimized is to learn to accept things you cannot change and focus on what is working in your life.

How do you know when you are functioning with a victim mentality or if it's just situational frustration?

A victim is the person who, no matter what, always has it worse. Nothing makes that person happy, and his or her life is filled with one crisis after another.

Contrast that with the person who chooses to focus on the answers rather than dwell on the hardship. The situation may be similar to the victim: spouse is deployed, kids are sick, car breaks down. Real stuff, real issues, but instead of throwing a pity party, this person develops a plan, rallies battle buddies, and works toward a solution. Initially, empowered spouses may spend time wishing things were different, and may even feel sorry for themselves, but unlike victims, they stop the pity party before it gets started.

I will never suggest that you pretend it's all white picket fences and pretty flowerbeds. Sometimes things aren't pretty and just because you might have trouble with daily life at times, does not mean you are playing victim.

Exercise: *Recognize the Difference*

List three characteristics you might see in each.

The empowered spouse:

_____

_____

_____

The self-victimized spouse:

_____

_____

_____

What about you? What are the situations, such as deployments or family drama, that shift your thoughts and cause you to act more like a victim than an empowered person?

_____

_____

_____

Exercise: *Victim-ville Residence Test*

For each statement about yourself in the following chart, mark true, sometimes true, or false.

	True	Sometimes	False
1. When chatting with friends, I often discuss how hard my life is.			
2. If something goes wrong, I tend to beat myself up about it.			
3. When receiving advice from friends, I often dismiss what they are saying because they can't really get what I'm going through.			
4. When others put me down, it hurts me to the core of my being, and I feel bad.			

(continued)	True	Sometimes	False
5. I spend too much time thinking about my past mistakes and failures.			
6. Sometimes I discuss my challenges just to get sympathy or to see if anyone really cares.			
7. If I wasn't so busy with the kids, the job, my family, etc., I'd be able to do what I really want to do.			
8. I'd like to eat healthier and exercise. I just can't right now; I have too much going on.			
9. More often than not, I find myself saying and/or thinking things like: "I can't," "I'm not good at," "I'll never be able to _____."			
10. Other people cause me to feel the way I do. I would be a lot happier if they didn't make me feel bad or guilty.			
Totals			

Add Your Total Points:
True = 2 points, Sometimes True = 1 point, False = 0 points

Score Analysis

16-20 points: Victim-ville Resident. Brace yourself and the truth will set you free. Those of us who feel victimized often believe we have no control over our daily lives. We use our circumstances to gain attention or shift our responsibilities. We convince ourselves that what's taking place is someone else's fault. Living life this way keeps us stressed out, unhappy, and fearful. Make the choice to take full responsibility for all that is happening in your life, focus on what is going right, and choose to break out of the cycle of victimization, and soon you will be able to embrace military life in a whole new way.

11-15 points: Victim-ville Frequent Visitor. It's a slippery slope my friend, and if you don't take time right now to shift your thoughts and change your outlook on military life, you will quickly find yourself a resident. Try to fill your days with a little gratitude, seek out positive experiences, and stop talking about how hard your life is. Instead, show kindness toward another person and practice forgiveness. These simple shifts in your mindset and outlook will improve your life, and this new way of thinking will soon become second nature.

6-10 points: Victim-ville Occasional Visitor. Good news: you can stop this nonsense right now! Having a victim mentality is a learned behavior that, like any other bad habit, can be stopped. With a little focused attention to your thoughts, conversations, and attitude, you will be back on track in no time.

0-5 points: Keep up the great work of actively choosing thoughts and actions that keep you from falling into a victim mentality, and thank you for bringing a smile to our community!

Give Yourself a SNAP!

I learned a great trick that helped me shift my negative thoughts. I wore a rubber band on my left wrist and each time I thought or said something victim-like, I snapped the rubber band and replaced the negative thought or comment with something positive and empowering.

If I looked in the mirror and thought about my chubby thighs, SNAP! If I told the story of my kid getting in trouble just to participate in a "woe is me party," SNAP! When I exaggerated about the sales clerk with a bad attitude for effect, SNAP! The cool thing was that after a week or so of sore wrists, I began to focus on good thoughts. In a matter of weeks, I had moved out of victim-ville, and now I spend very little time visiting. Try it, and let me know if this trick helps you as much as it did me!

A victim mentality can start in a number of ways, some traumatic. Because of this, transitioning out of it is not always as easy as a snap on the wrist. You may need additional support and resources to address your specific situation. If you frequently feel blue, or have trouble going about your daily routine, you may want to talk to a health care professional. It may be an indication of depression or anxiety.

Ask For and Give Help

It's important to note that asking for help does not mean you are a victim. You should reach out for assistance when you need it, tap into the expertise of someone who has experience in your current challenge, and express your feelings, especially sadness, frustration, or anger.

Sometimes we aren't as strong as our neighbor or as perky as Peggy Sue, and that's okay. We all have different skill sets, and we can work together to grow and survive in a life that constantly throws us curve balls. Nevertheless, if you use your feelings or limitations as an *excuse* for why your life isn't working, or to manipulate others to help you do things you are fully capable of, that is victim behavior, and it robs you of your personal power.

~

A Glimpse of the Life

In one of the military spouse groups I am part of on Facebook, a fellow spouse posted that her husband was "yet again packing for the field," and she was having a hard time with it. She was tired. Her husband been gone four out of the last eight weeks, and the kids were struggling from the lack of structure and the constant roller-coaster ride of saying goodbye and welcoming their soldier home. Their entire routine was disrupted, and it was difficult for the whole family.

Typically, when one of our own is having a hard time, military spouses are the first to step up to the plate. We get what it's like when our service members are deployed and we have to be everything to everyone. We understand that sometimes a helping hand takes the sting out of a bad situation.

But instead of the "how can I help?" response I usually see, this spouse was bombarded with comments and questions that were anything but supportive. She was asked how long he would be gone. "This time one week" was her response.

To my surprise, here is the "support" she got:

"Oh, a week is nothing; mine has been gone for a month."

"Be glad he's not in Afghanistan like my husband."

"The kids will be fine, they just need to get used to it."

"Why are you complaining? It's a nice break. Mine has been home for months. I wish he went to the field."

Sadly, she later posted, "You guys are right, he could be deployed, what was I thinking? … sorry for being such a whiner!"

I just wanted to scream!

Sorry? How can she be sorry? She reached out and was told her concerns were invalid. No, he's not deployed, but that doesn't make field and training time any less of a challenge. In fact, sometimes it can be harder, because we may not access our tried and true coping strategies.

~

When service members are in and out of the field, spouses are caught in limbo. You can't act like all is normal; your service member is not home. But it's not the same as a deployment, either. You can't use the "I'm allowed to crawl into bed and cry for two days because he's just deployed" coping strategy. There are no "in the field" support programs. You don't get the perks of separation pay, daycare sanity hours, emotional prep time, or two weeks of leave when they come home to readjust. And to make it worse, you are saying "See you later" so often, it can feel rehearsed and impersonal.

The Facebook group spouse had nothing to be sorry for. Any separation is a challenge. Whether it's for a short time or a long one, just the fact that the service member is gone at all stinks. The worst part of this situation was that instead of making the situation better, her peers negated her feelings and questioned her abilities as a military spouse.

This isn't just in the military community; it's everywhere. How many times have you been on the receiving end of the statement, "Really, that's nothing compared to my day" after you shared a challenge you had. Wouldn't it be nice if, instead, the person listened to you talk about your tough day and asked if they could help make it less stressful?

The spouse who reached out on Facebook could have used some tips on how to help her kids, de-stress herself, or even just an "I understand, I've been there" encouragement.

We never know what someone else's breaking point is, and we don't know what it's like to walk in their shoes. When we don't compare another's situation with our own, we are better able to support one another in a positive way.

Guide End-of-Day Thoughts

Take a minute and think about the last few nights. How did you spend the moments before you drifted off? Where were your thoughts focused?

For a long time, when my head hit the pillow, I tossed, I turned, and I worried. I went over the next day's schedule and my to-do list. I thought about my kids, especially if they had a particularly tough day, and I wondered if my spouse was really okay or if he was still working through that last deployment. I rehashed my day, hoping and wishing I would have done things differently, been more productive, or just had a little more fun.

At a recent seminar, I learned that most people spend the last five minutes before going to sleep stressing over all the things that did or did not happen that day. But when our thoughts focus on all the junk of the day, we set ourselves up for a repeat performance the next day.

The speaker explained that the last five minutes of the day are critical to positively jump-starting a good tomorrow because the last thing we think about before going to sleep is the thing our subconscious works on all night long. As we sleep, our subconscious mind processes all that is going on in our life, affecting our attitudes, beliefs, and behaviors. The last five minutes of the day are the body's way of clearing our hard drive and reprogramming it for future reference. When we imagine things unfolding perfectly, we allow our mind to work on finding ways to bring good things into our life. By changing our thoughts right before we go to sleep, we actually rewire our mainframe and affect the way we receive data in the future, causing us to act from a different place.

> When we imagine things unfolding perfectly, we allow our mind to work on finding ways to bring good things into our life.

At first, the concept that changing the last five minutes of my day could somehow change my life seemed a bit too far-fetched. I couldn't see how something so simple could help me find a healthier balance in my life. I do believe that our thoughts create our reality, and I know it's important to think in a way that is aligned with what we want. But it wasn't until I proved it for myself that I understood how important our final thoughts of the day really are.

I tested the theory the next time my spouse went for a two-week stint in the field. Each night the week before he left, I focused on how simple the time would be. I envisioned peaceful mornings, easy bedtimes, and calm days spent reading a good book after a productive day of writing. The minute my mind drifted to any thought of chaos or potential mishap, I focused on something good. I was pleasantly surprised at the result—that field time was a breeze—and excited to find a simple technique that could make such a difference in my life.

When I started to spend the last five minutes of the day differently, my mind-set, business, and entire life shifted. I stopped worrying so much. I thought about what I could do rather than things that could go wrong. When I focused on good things before I went to sleep, I slept better, and I woke up with a totally different outlook on the world, excited to begin my day.

It can happen for you, too. The following exercise will help you get started.

Exercise: *Maximize Day's End*

This simple exercise helps you leave the end of the day on a positive note and set yourself up for a better tomorrow. It works because as we sleep our subconscious processes solutions and works on new ideas as it restores our energy.

Throughout your day, record anything that feels good, moves you toward a goal, or that you want more of in your life. Write these on an index card, keep track in your favorite electronic device, or write each day in a notebook. You will use your daily list each evening. It may look something like this:

1. Received a call from my daughter saying, "I love you."
2. Completed my to-do list.
3. Took a walk in the park and enjoyed the crisp fall air.
4. Went to exercise class and finished the workout!
5. Enjoyed a warm cup of tea.
6. Heard my favorite song on the radio.
7. Wrote out my personal and business goals.
8. Paid the phone bill.

After your evening routine and right before you turn off the lights to go to sleep, read over your list for the day. Remember how it felt to complete each item or receive good news or enjoy a special moment. Focus on that feeling. If at any time your mind begins to wander, or you begin stressing about the future or rehashing your day in a negative way, refer back to the list and focus on those good things. Over time, the exercise will get easier, and you will begin to focus on the positive things that happen in your life! Try it.

Great things that happened today:

_____

_____

_____

_____

_____

_____

_____

Update Your Right Side Up Plan

Turn to the "In the Moment: Your Right Side Up Plan" on page 131. Gather your thoughts about the information and ideas from this chapter. Reflect on how you can apply these ideas, along with your own strategies, to update your personalized Right Side Up Plan.

Chapter 3
Flush the Stress

Nothing in my civilian background compares to the very real, palpable, ever-present stress of being a military spouse. Deployments, TDY, PCSs—on top of regular life as wife, mom, chauffeur, family member, support system, and housekeeper—yes, the life of a military spouse is full of stress!

Each of the roles we play, and all that we deal with day in and day out, work together to create a perfect storm. Like a hurricane off the shores of Haiti, it starts out small and may not get our attention right away. However, with the right acceleration and the perfect conditions, the pressure starts to build. Before you know it, it's time to batten down the hatches, because real danger isn't far behind.

That's exactly what happened to me toward the end of my husband's first deployment. I wasn't paying attention and got blindsided by my perfect storm. Naive to all the stress and building pressure, I thought I was handling my first deployment like a pro. But before I knew it, I found myself smack dab in the middle of a health crisis I didn't see coming.

~

A Glimpse of the Life

My first few years as an Army wife, I had everyone, including myself, believing I was handling and thriving in our military life. Some would even say I was in the running for the Super Spouse award. I volunteered for the FRG group with my husband's unit, helped out at school, ran a successful business, spent time with friends, was a rockin' mom, went on dates with my husband, and even kept the house clean and the kids fed. Super Spouse extraordinaire … until it all fell apart one day while my husband was deployed.

It was a typical afternoon. I was grocery shopping at the commissary and my phone rang; it was my son's school. A panicked nurse asked if she could have my permission to call an ambulance for my son. Umm, YES!! I was dumbfounded actually, I mean, if you are thinking he needs emergency treatment, then why are you calling me? But, hey, in the moment, I just said, "Of course," left my cart in the middle of the isle, and ran to my car.

I arrived just before the ambulance, to find my son in a chair, semiconscious, unable to talk or recognize where he was or who I was. My otherwise healthy seventeen-year-old son was possibly having a stroke. I was miles away from any family, with my husband in Iraq, daughter ten hours away at college. While I had battle buddies who dropped everything to help, they weren't who I wanted or needed by my side right then. All I could do was put my big-girl panties on and stay on mission. My mission in that moment was to handle the crisis at hand with precision, strength, and focus.

Due to an error in the first hours at the hospital, tests were inconclusive for a stroke. Amid hospital stays and specialist visits, I held it together when talking with my husband so he could focus on keeping himself and his soldiers safe. I was military spouse extraordinaire. I was strong and focused, and I took care of my son.

Over the next few months, we saw multiple specialists to ensure he had no long-term effects. All was well. When the crisis averted, a fascinating thing happened: I fell apart. (Now mind you, at the time, it didn't feel fascinating. But in hindsight, I see it all so clearly now.)

I had been ignoring the quiet warnings: not feeling well, knowing something was a bit off. But dang it, I had to carry out the military spouse role. Or so I thought. My body, however, had enough of being ignored. I landed in the hospital with a dangerously high blood pressure and multiple red flags pointing to issues with my heart.

I was able to ward off an actual heart attack due to quick actions by the ambulance and emergency room team. I now take preventative medication.

The choice to not take care of myself during a crisis at an already stressful time is something I'll never do again. I still look on that experience as a wake-up call. A real life slap in the face to remind me that if I want to be the best spouse and mom I can be, I have to take care of myself. I have to make sure my basic needs are covered, and I have to put on my own oxygen mask before I take care of anyone else.

~

I share this story because, for years, I believed I could do it all and be everything to everyone. This experience taught me several valuable lessons. It taught me not only the importance of resilience (chapter one), but also that if I want to thrive as a military spouse, I had better develop effective ways to flush the stress. What I was doing wasn't working. And this military life stress was different from any other type of stress I had dealt with before.

So I began researching and experimenting and, over time, through a series of trials and a lot of errors, I developed five key strategies to reduce the stresses of military life.

- Make myself a priority
- Cut the YUCK from my life
- Surround myself with positivity
- Get moving
- Get spiritual

These five simple strategies helped me flush my stress. Each works by itself, but when applied together, the effect is exponential. Employing these strategies has allowed me to take control of not only my health, but all aspects of my life. They can work for you, too.

Make Yourself a Priority

I have always been good at taking care of those around me. I love feeling needed. However, after my wake-up call, I finally accepted that I had to make myself a priority. No more adding new volunteer positions without letting a different one go, and no more saying yes to someone because it was easier than dealing with the fallout of saying no. I gave myself permission to put my needs first and found that, in doing so, I became much happier and much less stressed.

Consider the last time you were first priority in your life. Was it today? Yesterday? Or long ago? It is so much easier to squeeze in one more thing or cross off that one last to-do on the list, but the result is the same; when you put your own needs aside, you eventually run out of steam.

Maybe you are the person who volunteers for that one-time event and gets sucked into heading the committee. Perhaps you've become the spouse who offers to help out with the neighbors' kids once in a while and finds herself with a house full on a regular basis. Maybe you have become the person people call to vent their frustrations.

With the following simple strategy, I was able to assess my priorities and uncover what patterns of behavior I had fallen into that kept me from taking care of myself. I listened to the conversations going on around me. I listened to my husband suggesting that I was trying to do too much. I listened to my children as they whined because they just wanted to go home.

Listening became the thing I did before doing anything else. Through the art of listening, I began to make myself a priority once again. That's right, listening. You know, that thing we learned to do way back in kindergarten but maybe quit doing as adults. Yes, listening was the key to beginning the process of taking back my life.

I didn't grasp this concept fully until a trusted friend explained that listening actually helps us identify situations that need our attention and stay away from situations we have no business being a part of. When we actually listen to what people say and compare that with what our gut tells us, we have all the information we need to make choices that won't add stress to our lives.

> *Through the art of listening, I began to make myself a priority once again.*

Many military spouses are helpers who don't hear what people are actually saying or asking. We get wind of an imminent problem and immediately jump in to fix it before we know all the facts or the actual need. In our desire to help, we fail to see that helping may actually increase our own stress.

Jumping in when it isn't necessary isn't healthy for anyone. When we stop listening to our personal needs and believe we have to fix things for others, we end up carrying their burdens, and our priorities are no longer recognized as important. The result: We end up resentful, and our stress increases. No one feels good, and no one wins.

Think about it. If we really learned to listen to the actual needs of others and balanced those needs with what's best in our own lives, we would not only reduce our own stress, but would help others in a healthy and empowering way.

~

A Glimpse of the Life

The final few months of my husband Geoff's yearlong deployment took a toll on me in so many ways. It taught me much about myself, my life, and all the things I didn't do well over the last few years.

I had spent time taking care of my father as he fought cancer.

There were moves, sending my daughter off to college, dealing with deployment, deaths in the family … the stuff life is all about. Through it all, I didn't take the time or make the effort to recharge my batteries.

The toll I paid wasn't about the deployment, it wasn't about being mom, it wasn't about any of the stuff that life put in my path. It was a build-up of putting myself and my own health on the back burner. While that's okay for a very short period of time, long term it doesn't work so well.

I'm a little (okay, maybe a lot) type A and like things to run just so. I have this thought that if I can control things, everything will be okay. For some silly reason, I felt that if I kept everything in order, pretended I was fine, and didn't think about all the fear and stress I was feeling, somehow the stress wouldn't be there.

Fear, stress, and yuck happen. It's not whether it will happen, it is how you deal with it that matters.

And for me, it mattered because I didn't deal with it.

Sure, I went through the motions of talking about dealing with it, as I drank way too much coffee, skipped exercise (I was too busy, you know), ignored my feelings, and worried about the safety of my husband and daughter, who were both away from home for the first time. If that wasn't enough, I forgot the all-important necessity of listening to that little interior voice that knows when things are awry.

My voice was screaming in my ear, and I just kept brushing it away like a pesky fly, until it was so loud I couldn't ignore it anymore. I was forced, kicking and screaming, to "go to my corner" for a much needed time out!

~

Make yourself and your health a priority. Take a time out at the first signs of distress, and know that if you aren't functioning optimally, you can't do what you are here to do. If you are stubborn like I was, and choose to ignore that pesky voice, it will catch up with you!

When I learned to really listen, I realized that helping others doesn't mean sacrificing myself. Now I help in a healthy way with an open and caring heart. Through the skill of listening, I am now able to identify the ways in which I can help without adding stress to my already-busy life.

<u>Exercise:</u> *Become a Priority*

Who is your number-one priority? Is it you?

_____

_____

If you are *not* your first priority, what prevents you from doing the things you really want to do for yourself?

_____

_____

_____

_____

What would you be doing differently if you were your number-one priority? How would your daily life and activities change?

_____

_____

_____

_____

When other military spouses or friends share a problem or challenge with you, what do you do? Do you make suggestions, encourage, and guide them to seek out resources and information, or do you try to solve the problem for them?

_____

_____

_____

_____

How often do you put your needs aside to help others? How does this make you feel? Does it increase or decrease your stress level?

_____

_____

_____

_____

List three things you can do today to shift your focus and give priority to your needs and desires.

_____

_____

_____

Cut the Yuck

Did you know that military service has been identified as the most stressful job today? It beat out jobs like fireman, air traffic controller, and the like. It's no wonder military spouses are stressed; we are married to people who are working the most stressful job out there.

When I feel stressed, my first reaction is to turn to caffeine, food, or compulsive cleaning to take the edge off. Other people choose alcohol or nicotine. We use this *yuck* to avoid or escape the challenges in our lives, hoping to find relief. In truth, these crutches only give us a temporary reprieve.

So what can you do if you find that your occasional bowl of Chunky Monkey is turning into a nightly tub or a glass of wine is becoming a frequent go-to strategy? What do you do when stress continues to drain you of your energy or cause you to lose sleep? You can find time to exercise and relax (more on this later). And you can eliminate the yuck from your life.

Yuck is defined differently for each person. For you, it may mean reducing caffeine or sugar from your diet, or distancing yourself from negative people. Only you know what needs to be cut in your life.

Cutting the yuck is a simple strategy that had an immediate and positive effect for me. My stress decreased, my health improved, and positive things began to unfold.

There are four yucks that, collectively, when reduced or cut from our lives, create more time for things we love and help flush our stress:

- Food and chemical crutches
- Negativity
- Worry and fear
- The unnecessary

Yuck #1: Food and Chemical Crutches (Caffeine, Sugar, Alcohol, Nicotine)

Okay, breathe. I'm not saying you can't wake up to some Folgers in your cup or have a glass of wine after a long day. I'm saying that if you stop using these things as a way to get through the daylight hours, you will feel so much better!

So often, when we are stressed or running on empty, we reach for the quick fix, the things that will help push us through or give us energy to keep going. We may be able to buy ourselves a few more hours, but we are actually causing more stress on our bodies by ignoring the fact that they are telling us to slow down.

Energy drinks, sodas, and even my favorite chai latte from Starbucks, all give us that short boost to "git-r-done." But they may also push us beyond our natural physical capacity until we crash. Likewise, the glass (or two) of wine to relax can dehydrate us and prevent a restful night's sleep.

When we cut (or cut down on) these crutches, we feel better. Trust me, I didn't want to believe it either, but within a week after I cut this kind of yuck from my life, things were different. From the first day, I was able to sleep better, eat better, and get more done. I didn't feel as stressed and crazed, either. By week's end, my energy level improved, and I was more productive. It was as if someone had taken a huge burden off my shoulders, and I could finally breathe just a little bit better. Sure, I still get my latte every Tuesday morning before Bible study, but I don't get it every afternoon just to make it through the day. Yes, I have a glass of wine once in a while, but I stop at one unless it's a special occasion. An added bonus of cutting (or decreasing) the yuck I hadn't expected is that I've noticed a bit more cash in my pocket. Instant stress reliever in my world!

What's the yuck in your life? Evaluate your habits, really look at all you are doing, and decide what needs to go.

Exercise: *Cut the Crutches*

Do your eating and drinking habits change when you feel stressed? Do you turn to sugar? Maybe you have a few extra cups of coffee or a candy bar for extra energy? Perhaps it's an extra glass of wine or piece of pie. In terms of what you eat or drink, what yuck could you cut?

_____

_____

_____

_____

_____

_____

Cutting things like caffeine, sugar, and nicotine can be a challenge. What can you do to ensure you have healthy alternatives and activities ready when you need them?

_____

_____

_____

_____

_____

_____

Yuck #2: Negativity

One of the biggest stressors military spouses face is negativity. There is always someone dealing with a crisis or engaged in complaining. It's easy to fall into the glass-half-empty mind-set.

When I was surrounded by users and energy suckers, I poked holes in everything, second-guessed my actions, and analyzed each situation, looking for all the things that could go wrong. When surrounded by people who whined and bitched about their challenges, I tended to focus on my challenges as well.

However, when I chose to look through a positive filter and surround myself with positive, supportive people, it changed my life. The greatest impact was on my relationships. Instead of stressing over the rude behavior of the kids hanging out in our neighborhood, I was inspired by the group of students who made a difference at a local food bank. Rather than listening to catty chat after an FRG meeting, I politely excused myself to spend time with my family or a friend.

Now, I strive to surround myself with people who are in awe of their surroundings, who capitalize on new opportunities, and who look for the good in all situations. When I surround myself with positive people, my outlook on life is incredible. I expect good and look for the lesson in any struggle that comes my way. Positive people help me expect life to work in my favor.

It was the choice to change the filter through which I experienced military life that made it better.

The people we surround ourselves with affect us in many ways. We influence one another on matters of religion, politics, and money, and share in each other's daily experiences. These people become our sounding board, give us opinions, and even judge what we do. More importantly, we interact with them and ask for their input. All of these things, in turn, affect our thoughts, influence our behavior, and support our choices. No wonder our parents were so worried about who we hung out with in high school.

It was the choice to change the filter through which I experienced military life that made it better.

Do the people in your life make you feel good about who you are? Do they support you in your dreams and goals? Do they encourage you to be the best spouse, parent, employee, and friend you can be? Or do they bring you down every chance they get? If you look around and all you notice is a sea of negativity, then it's time to make some new friends.

Seek out people who like being part of our military family. Follow positive people on social media. You will soon find that wherever you look, you will discover something new about this life that has value.

Exercise: *Surround Yourself With Positivity*

What areas of your life do you view through a negative filter?

_____

_____

_____

_____

_____

_____

Make a list of ten things that are going well in your life. Refer back to this list each time negativity creeps in so you can shift your focus to what is going right!

_____

_____

_____

_____

_____

_____

_____

_____

_____

List five people who support you and help you live a better life.

_____

_____

_____

_____

_____

Who are the people you need to spend less time with?

_____

_____

_____

The challenge for today is to make time to hang out with people who feed your soul, energize your body, challenge your mind, and make you feel good about yourself!

Make a list of three people you would like to spend more time with.

_____

_____

_____

List five activities, events, or fun things you can do to bring more joy into your life. Choose one of the people you want to spend more time with and ask them to join you.

_____

_____

_____

_____

_____

Yuck #3: Worry and Fear

I don't know one military spouse who hasn't had a sleepless night spent worrying. Our lives and the lives of so many of our friends are a constant reminder of things to fear.

The other night when a group of Army pals were debating the merits of various Yoda quotes, speculating on how they related to our lives, I listened. Though I've never been a huge *Star Wars* fan, the conversation was fascinating, and I was surprised that it gave me a whole new appreciation for this short, big-eared Jedi master. His words were full of insight that could be applied to my life.

It started with my husband telling someone, "Do or do not; there is no try." The discussion that took place about that short sentence led me to start looking for more Yoda-isms. I found what may become my favorite quote of all time:

"Fear is the path to the dark side.
Fear leads to anger. Anger leads to hate.
Hate leads to suffering."

It got me thinking about how many times since I became a military spouse fear has led me to the dark side. Fear has caused me to do things I never intended to do, and to react to life defensively. Fear has caused me to lose sleep, jump to conclusions, and stress myself out. When I read that quote, it was as if I could see the cycle of my military life perfectly. I realized that my fear had caused me much suffering, and that wasn't the way to live a happy, fulfilling life.

Most of what military spouses fear is really worry about what could happen. Not what is happening right now, rather a focus on one potential outcome. What if we didn't fear that single result, but allowed ourselves to be hopeful? Wouldn't our fear and worry lessen?

Learning to be hopeful was key to my ability to get a good night's sleep and become less stressed. It wasn't like I just flipped a switch and instantly my fear turned to hope, but finding quotes, articles, cartoons, and blogs helped me see things in a different way. It helped me lighten up and stop taking every moment so seriously and inspired me to chill out and be less fearful of what might come up.

Fear, anger, and hate never lead us to our dreams. They strip us of our power and prevent us from taking action. We must break the cycle of fear and worry if we want to stay away from stress and the darker side of life.

The next time you find yourself feeling fearful and spending time worrying about the what-ifs, think of Yoda and step away from the dark side. Peace will follow.

Exercise: *Contain Worry and Fear*

What are your biggest fears? What do you worry about that causes you to lose sleep? Are you playing the *what if* game or projecting your fears? How can you shift your focus and change your actions to alleviate those fears rather than feed them?

_____

_____

_____

_____

_____

_____

Yuck #4: The Unnecessary

Family, business, community—I used to have lists for my lists, and I was the first one to volunteer if I saw a break in my schedule. I took on way more than I needed to do.

My stress dramatically decreased once I started cutting unnecessary activities. I set boundaries, such as not allowing myself to say "yes" to something without giving myself twenty-four hours to think about it. I quit registering the kids for new activities unless we let go of a current activity. By limiting what I committed myself and my family to do, I helped our lives become more manageable.

Cut the unnecessary from your life, and create the time you need to live the life that's right for you.

Exercise: Let Go of the Unnecessary

Often, stress comes from having too much on your plate and being over committed, over extended, and over scheduled. Make a list of three things you can you let go of today so you have more time for yourself.

_____

_____

_____

When is it hardest for you to say "no"? How can you create better boundaries for yourself?

_____

_____

_____

Get Moving

Health gurus tell us to get active, get exercising, do something to get our blood flowing. It's good for our health and well-being. Experts share how important it is and how simple it is to make time in our lives. Anyone can do it.

Sometimes the last thing I want to do is add one more thing to my crazy busy life. I feel good when I exercise, but the prep and wrap-up messes up my routine. I mean it isn't *just* thirty minutes on the elliptical. Once I'm done, I have to shower, change, dry my hair, etc., and who has time for that? But if I'm honest with myself, the gurus are right. When I do what they tell me, my stress goes down, and my emotional well-being improves.

Getting moving isn't about intensive training for a half marathon or hours at the gym. It can be as simple as stretching when you don't have time for anything else. It doesn't have to be on par with a service member's physical training regimen. Even if it's just fifteen minutes a day doing yoga or taking a walk, it's important to find something to get those endorphins (feel-good neurotransmitters) popping.

Exercise not only helps your body feel good, it also helps your mind. When you don't move your body, your mind doesn't have enough oxygen and blood flow to function optimally. Incorporating movement and activity into your daily routine sets you up to be more focused and productive. Regular exercise helps you interact more positively and cope better when things don't go as planned. Remember, exercise doesn't have to be intense, it just needs to be consistent.

Some great ways to get moving:

- Practice yoga (my all-time favorite)
- Walk/jog/run
- Take an exercise class

- Play hide-and-seek with the kids
- Follow along with a recorded routine
- Move to a YouTube video
- Park farther from the door at the commissary, mall, or school building
- Take the steps instead of the elevator
- Dance to favorite music
- Stretch
- Do five minutes of sit-ups, push-ups, and jumping jacks in between emails/edits/posting
- Hike
- Swim
- Bike to the library/commissary/exchange
- Meet the kids at the bus and walk home with them

Make exercise a priority, make it fun, and watch your stress melt away. You'll have more energy, and your favorite jeans might begin to feel a little looser. Now how cool is that?

Exercise: *Just Do It!*

What exercise or activity do you participate in regularly?

_____

_____

_____

What types of physical activities make you feel good?

_____

_____

_____

What are some of the challenges that keep you from being more active or maintaining a regular exercise routine?

_____

_____

_____

What are three activities you can spend less time doing so you can carve out more time to get moving?

_____

_____

_____

Taking into account all of the above—your current exercise routine, physical activities you enjoy, challenges, and small amounts of time in your schedule you can shift from other activities, create a plan for the next week to help you shift your habits to a more active lifestyle:

_____

_____

_____

_____

_____

_____

Get Spiritual

Military life is unpredictable, and there will be times you must find strength you may not think you have. This type of strength can be found by focusing on something bigger than yourself. I am talking about something very personal: faith.

Embracing spirituality takes stress relief to a whole new level. I see spouses who are going through the most intense struggles find peace through prayer. I see service members working with their chaplains, overcoming the sights and horror they experienced. I see families come together to work through crisis as they turn their lives over to a higher power. I see faith working in our community in so many ways. Faith got me through one of the most difficult moments in my life.

~

A Glimpse of the Life

My son seemed like the typical healthy nineteen-year-old attending college at Texas Tech University on various scholarships. He had friends, enjoyed the freedom, and seemed to be adjusting well, other than what I thought was a healthy dose of homesickness. My husband and I were settling into the empty nest, feeling we had "done good."

Then, on Oct 10, 2012, I received a call no mother wants to get, especially when you are helplessly too far away to hug your child … "Mom, I'm not okay, I need help."

This wasn't the "I procrastinated on my paper, and I need help to meet the deadline" type of call. It was the kind of call that brings you to your knees in an instant. In that moment, my world crashed in around me, my baby wasn't okay … he really wasn't okay.

After listening to my son, I realized his life was in danger. My ray of hope was that he did call me, he reached out for help. I quickly made a series of phone calls to the university and medical facility to get him to a treatment center. I got there as soon as they would let me visit him.

Only after he was in the treatment center did we realize how close we had come to losing him. He had been taking Adderall for his ADD. We had not seen any signs of substance abuse. I thought he was simply homesick. But he was diagnosed with mild depression, PTSD, and prescription drug and alcohol addiction.

I felt so much guilt because I hadn't seen it coming. How did I not see it? The reality was that my son didn't want me to see it. Like many other PTSD and depression sufferers, he kept his struggles to himself in a silent, personal torment.

God was with me the day my son called, a day when my husband was away on temporary duty with no means of communication. During my son's journey through treatment and recovery, I learned what it meant to really depend on my faith. I let go and let God lead us.

My son is better now. In fact, he shares his story and allows me to share our journey with the hope it will help others who fight depression, addiction, and suicidal thoughts. For me, it was the first time I truly understood the role of faith.

~

So often when life isn't going well, people question whether or not there is a higher power at all. My strength comes from my faith. The challenges I've faced as a military spouse have been easier to work through because of the depth of my spiritual life. I know my God can do anything. When I was ten hours away from my child in crisis, I looked to a power much greater than myself for strength and peace of mind.

My trust in God began when I was eleven years old and my six-month-old baby brother died. We all were so sad, angry, and confused. I remember asking God to help me understand, to help me help my family. With the faith of a child, I turned it all over, and I was never alone in my grief. There was a strength that rose up within me that wasn't my doing. Sure, there are scars and sadness that remain, but my spiritual foundation, my faith, helped me then and continues to help me today.

It's been my experience that the lives of people who trust in God (or their own version of a higher power) are far less stressful than those who have no faith at all. I believe you can get through anything if faith is the center of your life.

I am not telling you how to believe or trying to convert, save, or preach to you. Nor am I trying to tell you how to practice your spirituality. No matter where you are in your spiritual journey, I encourage you to dig deeper.

Situations military spouses deal with require us to carry on even when we aren't sure we have it within ourselves to do so. By gaining strength from something greater than myself, I am reminded that my life and the struggles I face have purpose and meaning.

What fills you up spiritually? Is it reading the Bible, starting your day in prayer, or connecting with a faithful community? Maybe it's taking a class or spending time in nature. Whatever works for you, do it. Growing your faith is a key strategy that can help you get a clear picture of your life and cope with the challenges. Faith is a source of strength when things get tough and can create a peace in your heart, mind, and soul.

Exercise: *Connect Spiritually*

From where do you draw your strength?

_____

_____

_____

_____

_____

When do you feel truly at peace? Is it when you are alone in a quiet place? Walking in the woods? Reading scripture? Writing in your journal?

_____

_____

_____

_____

What helps ground and renew you so you can focus on all the good life has to offer?

_____

_____

_____

_____

What can you do to enhance your spiritual journey or improve your relationship with God or your higher power?

_____

_____

_____

_____

_____

_____

Update Your Right Side Up Plan

Turn to the "In the Moment: Your Right Side Up Plan" on page 131. Gather your thoughts about the information and ideas from this chapter. Reflect on how you can apply these ideas, along with your own strategies, to update your personalized Right Side Up Plan.

Chapter 4
Respond to Change

There is no shortage of change in the military lifestyle. Embracing change is perhaps the biggest hurdle I faced in my first few years as a military spouse. I struggled with the fact that I never knew what to expect. I hated that I had no idea what Uncle Sam would ask of us next, and I coped the only way I knew how, which was to prepare for every possible scenario, just in case. I always felt like I was waiting for the ball to drop, and I longed for consistency.

Sure, I knew that change was inevitable. I even expected it, but my heart had a hard time accepting the fact that our lives weren't our own anymore.

Eventually, I was able to develop coping strategies by shifting my mind-set and refining my expectations. I stopped feeling the need to prepare for every possible scenario and began to live with a simpler go-with-the-flow approach. I became less afraid and more confident in my ability to handle challenges as they came up. I learned how to thrive while living in the moment.

~

A Glimpse of the Life

Change is a regular part of my life now. I get that. But man-oh-man, this past year has been filled with too much of it, and frankly, I would like a time out so I can adjust a bit.

I find I can best deal with change if I know it's coming. However, when the change is unexpected, or even a tad on the emotional side, it takes me longer to find my bearings and get back into the routine of my life. Good change, bad change, any kind of change temporarily prevents me from functioning at my peak.

Things like my baby going off to college, welcoming a new son-in-law into the family, celebrating the fact we're going to be grandparents, moving to a new assignment in Colorado ... all of these things are GOOD things, but each one of them means an adjustment. Put them all together and, well, the realm of Judy-ville is under a severe storm warning.

With so many changes occurring in such a short period of time, I feel off and disconnected. I have a huge need to take some time to settle into the newness, but truthfully, who really has time for that? Military life doesn't stop just because life gets hectic and full.

I find myself thinking, I "should" do this, or it "would" be better if I had done that, and all the ways I "could" have handled it but didn't. Oh, the shoulda, woulda, couldas ... take over my life. I feel like I'm in the spin cycle of a washing machine, and I don't know how to stop.

Instead of giving myself enough time to come to terms with the fact that things aren't the same, I pressure myself into thinking I am supposed to know how to deal with it *pronto*. I'm not that together!

When my son left for college, it took me months to change my grocery routine. Over and over, I'd get to the check out and have to take back the Oreos and the chips (okay, truth be told, chips often stayed in the cart, but the Oreos actually went back to the shelf). It took me even longer to enjoy the quiet and not hear every unfamiliar noise and wonder what it was without stressing out.

I am still adjusting to my daughter being married. I'm happy for her and the man she loves, but everything is changing so quickly, it's not easy. And military life just keeps going on amidst everything else.

These changes mean that my life is different. Not bad different, just different, and I have to adjust.

~

Embracing change is a process we master over time. It isn't a skill that is bestowed upon us, rather it is something we learn little by little, through experience.

As I progress in my ability to accept and respond to change, I'm realizing that change, while it happens in an instant, is just the start of a process that continues on and becomes part of everyday life. Change does not have a definitive conclusion, and there is no one right way to handle a particular situation. We all experience things in our own way and in our own time, and some strategies to embrace change work better than others.

Whenever change looms, whether a deployment, move, baby, death, or anything else, I find myself wanting to be in command of everything around me. I want things to fit my personal agenda, and I resist taking action unless the new situation is something I'm comfortable with. I want life to unfold how I think it should.

Some situations I have the ability to take charge of, while others are beyond my control. By understanding and accepting that reality, I can better accept change and embrace the process of moving through it.

The last time my husband returned from a two-month assignment, he was finally supposed to be home for a while. Only a week had gone by since his return, when duty called once again. My husband and I know each other almost better than we know ourselves, and I can tell you the last thing he wanted to do was dump another unexpected change onto my lap. It had been a chaotic and intense year, and he was nervous about how I would handle the news. My reaction surprised us both.

The simple mind-set shift of understanding what part of the change process I had control over, and what I didn't, helped me understand that leaving again would be just as hard for him. I was able to accept that the assignment was out of my control, but how I handled it was something I did have power over.

Looking at change as a process rather than an event helped me see that the orders were only the catalyst that began the process. I could, through trial and error, find ways to handle it better this time around.

Change, while it happens in an instant, is just the start of a process that continues on and becomes part of everyday life.

The first hint of impending change used to bring feelings of panic, anxiety, anger, and even fear. But when I stopped looking at change as a single action or instantaneous event, I began to see it in a more positive light. That single action wasn't nearly as scary as all the possible unknowns I had no control over anyway.

In my civilian life, I was the kind of person who loved change. Change was motivating and always felt like an adventure. But it was less frequent than the change of military life. As a military spouse, I longed for routine and consistency, and I started to feel like change was a punishment.

But the change that occurs in military life is an unavoidable reality that doesn't have to run or ruin our lives. In fact, it can do just the opposite; it can open doors, as long as we have the right mind-set and attitude toward it.

It took a while before the shift in my attitude made a difference in my world. This shift helped me refine my expectations and look at my life in a much more positive way. I learned new coping skills and gained wisdom that helped me land right side up. I stopped focusing on the inconvenience of change and embraced the process in a way that made me stronger and brought our family closer together.

Adopt the ARA Process

Time and again, my experiences (often likened to a whack on the head with a two-by-four) have taught me that change can be a rewarding experience—if I allow myself a bit of wiggle room. When I let myself be flexible and try not to fight what's happening, change becomes an opportunity to take the reins and choose what I want to do differently in my life. For me, change is a time when I can redefine who I am and put my past (and the mishaps that inevitably occurred) behind me.

Knowing I have the power to make the most of any situation helps me navigate tough circumstances much more successfully. You can, too, using what I call the ARA process. This process allows me to move from emotional freak-out and paralyzing fear to focused action. It's as simple as:

- Accept
- Regroup
- Approach

Accept

Learning to accept change (or accept what you can't change) is the first step in learning how to fully function within a life of constant change. Acceptance can mean the difference between coasting through change and being overwhelmed by it. Accepting inevitable change does not necessarily mean you agree with a change or want it, or that you are giving up on other possibilities. When you accept the situation, you give yourself a framework within which to work out *your* plan to *respond* to the change and to continue to live your life fully despite the continuing change around you.

It used to be a challenge for me to plan anything beyond what to make for dinner. A last-minute hiccup could turn life on its ear, so "why even bother to plan" was my plan. That is, until I realized we really weren't getting anywhere, and each of us felt like we had no control or optimism for our future.

At times, I felt that if I planned for the future, I might jinx my husband's safety. I felt that if we only focused on this moment, somehow I would be able to control our lives and everything would work out perfectly. The joke was on me. I discovered that this way of life left me with a lot of questions I had no answers to, questions that mattered a lot.

How would our kids pay for college? Where would we go once we left the military? What would happen if an injury caused a medical discharge? These questions and so many others were always somewhere in the back of my mind, but I never allowed myself to actually seek out the answers. Why? Because I knew in my gut that the life and future of any service member is very unpredictable—a reality too painful and scary for me to think about.

Then one day, I heard a Gold Star wife speak about her experience and how she handled the loss of her active duty husband. I realized that I was living my life in fear. I was protecting myself. Among the many pearls of wisdom she shared that day, one comment stood out. She said that when we ignore or dismiss the fact that our loved ones have chosen a career that puts them in danger, we are doing ourselves harm. Acceptance of that fact was something which, until that point, I was unable to fathom.

As she spoke, I realized that I had given in to the idea that being in the military meant we couldn't have a future. WOW, how wrong I was!

Hearing that speaker—someone who had hit her greatest fear with full force—made me see that I had to stop avoiding and ignoring change. I saw the importance of separating the things I could control from the things I couldn't. I needed to quit trying to manage every aspect of my life and allow change to become an integral part of it all. Most importantly, I realized the way I had been dealing with military life was preventing me from embracing all that was before me.

When I got home, I sat down with my husband and shared with him my concerns and fears. I told him I needed his help to understand what I do and don't have control over. Together, we took what I learned from the Gold Star wife and applied it to our life. Little by little, I began to embrace the idea that military life was our future, changes and all, and with help I could find my way.

Accepting the challenges of military life can help you manage, plan, and live *your* life no matter what changes come your way. Think of acceptance as a muscle. You need to pay attention to it and work with it so it can handle what you ask it to do.

Exercise: *Visualize Acceptance*

Use this exercise whenever unexpected change comes into your life. It is part of the change process that will help you let go of the fear and stress that surrounds the circumstances that come up in military life.

Describe a recent (or soon-to-be) change in your life.

_____

_____

_____

_____

_____

_____

What is your physical reaction to this change? Does your heart race, face flush, shoulders tense, breath become shallow? Write down five physical characteristics you experience with this change.

_____

_____

_____

_____

_____

Often our thoughts and feelings about any type of change are worse than the change itself. Take a moment to examine the thoughts going through your mind. Are they building fear or empowering you to move through the change?

_____

_____

_____

_____

Are you accepting or fighting this change? Is your instinct to protect yourself? What are you avoiding or ignoring so you don't have to deal with the situation?

_____

_____

_____

_____

_____

_____

Now that you are aware of how you are currently feeling about the situation, you can let go of the struggle by following these steps.

- Find a quiet place away from distractions.

- Close your eyes and visualize walking into a room that has a table in it with a huge bowl on top.

- Look at your hands. You are carrying a plate full of your feelings and thoughts. On this plate are all the things preventing you from accepting the changes in your life and stopping you from embracing the opportunities.

- Slowly walk to the table and, one by one, place each of the things on your plate into the bowl. Take each item, emotion, and action, and visualize yourself moving each from your plate into the bowl. Allow yourself to feel the weight of each item as you drop it in. Hear the sound it makes. Allow the feelings to leave your body as you place them into the bowl. Continue until your plate is empty.

- Look at everything you have been carrying and allow yourself to let it go. Visualize yourself physically turning around and walking away, acknowledging that you no longer have anything preventing you from moving into the space of open acceptance.

Regroup

The next step in the ARA process is essentially a crash course in six strategies that changed my life. Prior to discovering these, if things were challenging, I would utter the phrase *"I'm done!"* more often than not. Done trying, done being disappointed, done eating cold meals because of someone else's timeline, just done.

When I began to recognize my own personal growth, personalize the advice I received, and allow myself the luxury of a do-over, my life began to shift. I developed tools based on my experiences without being consciously aware of it. As a result, I was able to accept that change goes hand in hand with military life, and I could see how embracing change would open up new opportunities for me. Through the process of regrouping, I was able to make a fresh start.

Regrouping gives you perspective to see where *you* fit into the changes and choices in your life, and how you can best respond to and take advantage of your situation to create an even better one.

Strategy #1: Acknowledge You Are Growing Stronger

One of the most important benefits to dealing with change is that, as you move through it, you are also learning new skills. Each challenge you overcome helps you gain confidence and develop and grow as a person, eventually coming to a point where you are able to do things you never thought were possible.

I didn't acknowledge any of these benefits at first; in fact, I didn't see any good at all in living the military life day in and day out. I couldn't understand how anyone could be expected to handle all that I was juggling, and it really ticked me off. Then, just before another last-minute TDY goodbye, a longtime friend remarked at how differently I was handling things. She pointed out that I was calm and proactive instead of dizzy and unfocused. Funny that she was the one who saw I had become a stronger, more resilient spouse *way* before I did.

That simple observation triggered something within me and gave me a new appreciation for all I had been through. The changes taking place were actually having a positive effect on my life. I began to understand that walking through the ick was actually worth it. In that moment, I realized that no matter what came up, the ability to handle it and land on my feet at the same time was within me. It was a turning point in my feelings toward being a military spouse.

Who would have thought that the changes I had been resenting for so long would help me become a better person, better wife, and better friend? Change forced me out of my comfort zone and helped me gain confidence in my ability to handle new situations. Acknowledging the good that came from what I had been through was an important first step in developing a new perspective of military life.

> Who would have thought that the changes I had been resenting for so long would help me become a better person, better wife, and better friend?

Strategy #2: Ignore the False Alarm

Since the beginning of time, humans have exhibited a natural survival instinct, responsible for keeping us safe from harm. An internal alarm sends us a warning from deep within our gut whenever our environment changes drastically or danger is present. This natural defense is essential to our overall survival. But sometimes, that alarm can give a false warning when there is actually no danger present.

Understanding how to tap into this natural survival instinct while ignoring the false alarm is the second strategy in regrouping.

When my daughter was a teenager, she wasn't equipped to handle the constant changes brought on by my husband's choice to rejoin the military. Anytime plans changed, she threw herself into fight-or-flight mode. Her instincts falsely told her she was in danger. In an attempt to cope, she tried to control everything around her. I quickly realized we had to find ways to make her feel safe and secure once again.

Establishing a clear, predictable routine helped her relax and return to her fun-loving, happy self. She even found ways to enjoy the military experience. She joined JROTC to learn the military lingo and meet other military kids. She worked out at the gym on post and acclimated herself to the pulse of a military base. It was nothing major, but several little effective adjustments worked wonders and calmed the danger alerts her body was sending out.

It's natural for our bodies to physically react to new situations, especially life threatening ones. For the most part, being a military spouse doesn't fit into the life threatening category. However, as in my daughter's case, sometimes the signals in our minds and bodies get crossed. Only after she had enough positive experiences to associate with the changes could her mind connect to the idea that she was safe. By going through these safe and positive experiences, she was able to silence the alarms and allow herself the opportunity to deal with change in a healthy and proactive way.

Strategy #3: Filter and Personalize Advice From Others

During our first permanent change of station, I wanted to educate myself about what pitfalls to avoid in the move. So I sought out my battle buddies who had been through the process a number of times. I received advice about color coding, packing, avoiding a delayed travel voucher, and much more. However, much of the input I received didn't apply to our situation. Like a good soldier, I followed rank and implemented each idea as best I could. But rather than create a smoother transition to our new installation, the result was a system I had no idea how to decode, and I was left searching for what I needed for a very long time.

Ask, listen, filter, personalize.

This experience taught me that the way I would tackle a PCS was different from my friends' approach. Their way left me eating off paper plates for weeks.

Asking for advice was a big part of my initiation process, but I learned that while it is important to ask for advice when you need it, it is just as important to listen and implement that advice with a *what's best for me* filter. Approaching things this way allowed me to collect ideas and information, learn from others, and use it to develop a system that works well for our family. Ask, listen, filter, personalize.

Strategy #4: Start Fresh

Starting fresh is my favorite strategy. It's one of those military life benefits few people talk about, but I am grateful for. With each change or new set of orders, I feel as though I have been given a blank slate, with permission to discard anything that isn't working in my life and replace it with something better. It's an opportunity to get rid of the clutter, tired ideas, old routines, and negativity, and start anew.

This strategy came to me when we left our first duty station. There, I had surrounded myself with all the wrong people and lost myself in the process. As we pulled out of El Paso, Texas, and headed to our new home, it occurred to me that I had the unique opportunity for a do-over. Never before had I answered my husband's "Are you ready?" louder than on that day. With a resounding "HOOAH!" we set out with a chance to make things better. I was so grateful to hit that big fat reboot button.

Having the ability to take all I had learned in those first few years, regroup, and start over felt amazing. It gave me the opportunity to become the military spouse I longed to be: strong, resilient, positive, and most of all, able to embrace change as it occurs in my life.

Strategy #5: See Endless Possibilities

As military families, we can travel the world, meet people of every economic and social background, and try a wide variety of cuisine. Our children often become multilingual, with an acceptance of differences in others that makes us proud. When we start to see the possibilities rather than the roadblocks, we think bigger and begin to see potential where before we saw only limitations.

After I finally got to the point where change didn't freak me out or knock me flat on my backside, I realized that the act of embracing change could create endless possibilities. A new start, a new job opportunity, and new experiences—it was all right there in front of me.

When looking at change from a place of possibility, there is no room for fear or anxiety. The confidence that comes from viewing life this way pushes me to try things I had not allowed myself to do before.

One day during my husband's first deployment, I took myself on a date. I went to my favorite restaurant alone. Never in my life had I dined without company. Walking in and telling the hostess I wanted a table for one was uncomfortable. I ordered, people-watched, and took it all in. I allowed myself to be open to the experience. Much to my surprise, I loved it and I now take myself out regularly.

Endless possibilities come when we learn to explore new situations and allow ourselves to grow into them. Thinking about change from the perspective of a *positive what if* opens our minds to more of what could be.

Strategy #6: Be Bigger, Bolder, Brighter

To claim our power over the challenges that change can bring, we need to be:

BIGGER in the way we seek out opportunity,

BOLDER in the way we go for what we want, and

BRIGHTER in the way we see our future.

Imagine how we could embrace the change that comes our way if we fill our thoughts with hope, knowing that all we ever dreamed of or wished for is possible.

I don't have the kind of power to prevent tragedies, but what I do have is the ability to think bolder and push myself toward a better life. I can let go of the negative what if questions and focus on a bigger game where I can create and experience life the way I want to live.

This shift in thinking helped me step out of my comfort zone and write this book. The math major in me had never considered the possibility of writing a book until I began to think with a bigger, bolder, and brighter mind-set. Instead of dismissing the idea, I took a chance and decided to share my story in an effort to help others. If I hadn't allowed myself to focus on the endless possibilities, I would have allowed fear and doubt to prevent me from helping others learn better ways to deal with change and the stress and chaos that goes with military life.

Exercise: *Regroup*

Describe specific ways that change has helped you grow.

_____

_____

_____

In what situations do your natural defenses send off false alarms? What triggers set them off?

_____

_____

_____

List three pieces of advice you have received that have helped you along the way.

_____

_____

_____

Describe a time when listening to someone else's advice did not serve you well. How could you have better filtered or personalized the advice for your life?

_____

_____

_____

How and when do you want to start fresh? What's preventing you from doing that now?

_____

_____

_____

_____

What are some of the endless possibilities, goals, and dreams that are now open to you?

_____

_____

_____

_____

_____

_____

What can you do to begin to embrace change and think of it as an opportunity rather than a hassle?

_____

_____

_____

_____

Approach

Service members, while on mission, are forced to deal with unexpected situations all the time. Not only do they need to meet their objectives, but they must do so with a whole new set of challenges they may not have expected.

Military spouses also have to adjust on the fly due to unforeseen changes in plans. If we accept our new situation and take a moment to regroup, we can approach change rather than run from it, allow the change to take place with the least amount of interference as possible, and manage our response to the change.

When a situation is completely new or unfamiliar, this process can be difficult. Circumstances like another change of duty station or preparing for deployment take a bit more effort. We can't just let the chips fall where they may, but we can approach the situation differently by first looking at the facts and evaluating our options before taking action.

To effectively approach and respond to change, we need to:

- Look at the facts
- Evaluate our options
- Decide how to proceed

Look at the Facts

When faced with change, rather than submerging in busy work, procrastinating, or flipping out (all of which I've been known to do), it's important to set aside emotions for a moment and gather the facts of the situation.

Search online, ask questions, research, and make lists to uncover information that will help you adjust in a proactive way. What are the details: who, what, where, when? What other changes may follow? What can you find out about those changes? For example, if you are moving to a new duty station, what can you find out about schools, doctors, churches, weather, possible job transfers for yourself, and other information that will help you plan and know more about the effect of the change?

Evaluate the Options

It took time before I could appreciate the idea that finding my way through any military situation was all about understanding I had options. It wasn't about knowing the right or perfect thing to do; it was about accepting that it was okay when I didn't have all the answers, and being confident and willing to seek out alternative solutions.

When we arrived at our first duty station, we had been told there was a house waiting for us, and we were eager to get settled. I hadn't yet learned of the "it's not a go until it goes" philosophy, so when we got to the housing office and we were told there was nothing available, my world came to a standstill. I couldn't hold back the tears.

When I quit crying long enough to gather some facts, I was able to put things into perspective. We didn't become homeless that year, and everything eventually worked out to our advantage, but only after I allowed myself to take a step back and see that we had options that actually better suited our needs.

Lack of housing, a messed-up LES, or an unexpected flat tire doesn't have to turn your world upside down, if you know you have options. Canceled plans, late dinners, and missed appointments don't have to bring you down, if you know you have choices. Recognizing you have alternatives is empowering. It means you are not trapped by your circumstances. With the facts, information, and choices in front of you, it's easier to calmly choose the best one.

Decide How to Proceed

The old Judy had a hard time deciding how to proceed and what action to take. My mind was like a gerbil on its wheel, going round and round, worrying about all the things that could go wrong. I stressed about my ability to handle the situation as it presented itself. And once I took action, I stressed about whether or not I made the correct decision.

I eventually came to understand that deciding how to proceed is actually the simplest part of the entire process. I have the facts, I've looked at the choices, so all that's left is to pick the option that makes the most sense in that particular moment of my life, and do it. It's like choosing an outfit. Is it comfortable? Is it right for the occasion? Does it make me feel good? Then, yes, it's a winner.

The best options feel right. Like our clothes, we can always change them if they aren't working for us anymore. So when it's time to choose, start with the option that feels good. Don't worry if it's not perfect. You can always regroup and try again. No choice is wrong; some choices take a bit more time and offer you a different experience. Deciding how to proceed allows you to start the momentum. You can always go back to gather more facts and adjust as you go.

Exercise: *Approach Change*

Describe a change you are facing.

_____

_____

_____

_____

_____

What experience do you have with changes like this?

_____

_____

_____

List the important facts and information available.

_____

_____

_____

_____

What are your options for how to handle this change?

_____

_____

_____

_____

Which option makes the most sense logically and emotionally? Which option feels best?

_____

_____

_____

_____

Refine Your Expectations

There are two kinds of expectations: realistic and unrealistic. Realistic expectations can motivate and inspire us to move through change in a positive way; they can help us gauge another person's motives and intentions and help us learn how to improve our lives. However, unrealistic expectations set us up for disappointment.

I remember one year when my mother and father decided to try a different vacation idea. Instead of our usual family excursion, the boys would go with Dad on a fly-in fishing trip, and the girls would go for a spa weekend. My father built it up in his mind to be an incredible bonding experience where he and his sons would have meaningful guy talk and create memories for a lifetime. They had a great time, but the trip didn't quite measure up to what my dad had imagined. His unrealistic expectations were based on what he believed an eleven- or twelve-year-old boy would think was fun. He didn't ask or involve my brothers; he made adult assumptions, and it almost ruined the trip.

When our expectations are different from what actually transpires, we become disappointed.

Unrealistic expectations come from our beliefs about how we think someone should feel or act. When our expectations are different from what actually transpires, we become disappointed. If my dad had gone on that trip with no expectations about how things would unfold, he could have lived in the moment and enjoyed learning what his sons liked to do. Instead, he placed his agenda onto their lives and was disappointed when what he thought would happen was very different from what actually did happen.

~

A Glimpse of the Life

When I first came into the military, I had expectations that my family and lifelong friends would be my best support system. They knew me best, and I thought they could help me through deployments and the changes military life brings just as they had helped me through other challenges throughout my life.

Around month four of my husband's first deployment, my strength was wishy-washy to say the least, and I was tired of missing my spouse and worrying for his safety. I had just had a birthday that passed quickly without fanfare, and I was homesick. I wanted to spend time with our friends who had celebrated with me over the years. Plus, I was married and it just didn't seem fair that I was celebrating without my soldier.

I called a nonmilitary friend to talk it out and get the support I "expected" from her. After fifteen minutes of chit chat, she asked if she could be honest with me, and then said something I will never forget. She said, "Judy, what did you expect when he enlisted? You knew he would deploy. I don't see why you sound so surprised that it's hard now that he's gone and you are alone."

In that instant, a few things hit me, and I'm not sure which was worse: The fact that she was right, or the fact that I realized she couldn't be the support system I needed when my soldier was away. My expectation that she could empathize with my new life left me frustrated and full of disappointment, and it wasn't fair to her.

I vowed to change the expectations I had for my civilian family and friends. They love me, and they care about me and my family when we are going through challenges, but they can't empathize as I want them to. They don't know what to say when military life rears its ugly head. I'm being selfish to think they should. Only someone who has walked in my shoes can know when it's time to kick my ass and hand me a pair of big-girl panties versus when it's time to cry with me and share in the knowledge that sometimes this military life stinks.

~

The more realistic your expectations, the easier it will be to roll with the changes. Being able to let go of unrealistic expectations will stop you from setting yourself up for disappointment and allow you to fully embrace the realities of military life in a new way.

Exercise: *Reset Expectations*

This exercise will help you walk through a situation and determine whether or not the expectations you have affect your ability to enjoy the situation. By looking at what you expect and what actually occurs, you can see how your expectations play a part in your experience.

Think about an upcoming event, such as a birthday, anniversary, outing, or trip. What would make it perfect? Who would be there? What does it sound like, look like, feel like? How would everyone act and interact? Describe the scene in a way that you could look back and say everything turned out perfectly.

What do you *expect* this same event to be like? How does what you expect to happen differ from what you hope for in an ideal situation?

———————————————————————————

———————————————————————————

———————————————————————————

———————————————————————————

———————————————————————————

———————————————————————————

After the event takes place, reflect on your experience. Were you happy? Was it what you expected? Hoped for? What actually happened and how did the outcome differ from your expectations?

———————————————————————————

———————————————————————————

———————————————————————————

———————————————————————————

———————————————————————————

———————————————————————————

———————————————————————————

Describe what you expected of yourself and the other people involved. Did the reality of everyone's behavior differ from what you thought it would be? How did you behave? Did these behaviors make or break the event's success?

_____

_____

_____

_____

Did your expectations affect your ability to enjoy the moment? Did your expectations impact how you felt before, during, and after the event?

_____

_____

_____

_____

_____

Update Your Right Side Up Plan

Turn to the "In the Moment: Your Right Side Up Plan" on page 131. Gather your thoughts about the information and ideas from this chapter. Reflect on how you can apply these ideas, along with your own strategies, to update your personalized Right Side Up Plan.

Chapter 5
Find Your Way

The minute my husband put on his uniform, it seemed as if my entire life and identity turned camouflage. I disappeared into the background and didn't have a clue where I was going. When it felt like life was becoming unmanageable, I began looking for the cause. Was it finances, my husband's job, his recruits? Was it the duty station, that particularly awful deployment, our relationship, or maybe all the above?

I spent countless hours searching for reasons why I felt lost, but I couldn't shake the feeling I was on a road going nowhere. If only I could put aside my ego and ask for directions, right? Asking for directions is an important part of finding your way as a military spouse. It can keep you from feeling lost and resentful, and instead steer you toward unique opportunities and adventures.

No one has all the answers. Even with all that I have learned, I'm not living completely stress free, nor am I Little Miss Judy Sunshine all of the time. I have to work at staying positive, and I have to maintain focus on my long term goals. I also have to remind myself to establish priorities and embrace this life just like everyone else does.

Prioritize

When you know what's most important, you can say "yes" to actions that support your top priorities and "no" or at least "not now" to everything else. Your daily choices—what you do, who you spend time with, where you focus your attention—should all align with what you want for your life, including your military life experience.

Prioritizing is not always that straightforward though. Military spouses tend to be extremely busy multitaskers. Many of us jump in feet first, figuring things out along the way. For the most part, that works. It may be one of our best coping skills. But if we jump without considering how it will impact our daily life, we've just contributed to the problem.

~

A Glimpse of the Life

My life is really busy. I try to balance multiple businesses with being a military spouse and mother, keeping up with the house and errands ... the list goes on. For weeks, I've felt like nothing ever gets accomplished.

Yesterday, I decided to be proactive and make a list of all the things I wanted to accomplish over the next forty-eight hours. Ten minutes and two pages later, my jaw dropped, and I laughed that "you have got to be kidding" sarcastic kind of laugh with eyebrows and mouth turned in opposite directions. Had I lost my mind? And who was I kidding? No one could accomplish that list even if they had a staff of five to help.

So I decided to do what the time management peeps tell me to do. I got busy prioritizing my list. But there was the real issue. I mean if I knew which thing was more important than the other, I wouldn't be in this situation now would I?

I tried to figure out what actually should take priority, and the answer that was stuck in my brain was ... well, EVERYTHING.

- Spend time with my family ... important
- Project #1 for my business ... important
- Project #2 for my business ... important
- FRG meeting ... important
- PCS paperwork ... important

- Facebook/Twitter ... important ☺
- Supporting/spending quality time with my service member ... important
- Taking care of the kids ... important
- Supporting my battle buddies ... important
- Volunteer work ... important
- Personal growth, Bible study ... important
- Time to relax/recharge ... important
- The housework ... I guess sort of important

The list went on and on, and for hours I just couldn't let anything go. It really made me wonder: If everything is always SO important, how can we possibly get anything done? More specifically, how can anyone do anything if we're always worried about something else? The simple answer: we can't.

~

No one can perform at peak, feel accomplished, or be truly happy if there's always something more important they feel they should be doing. At least I know I can't.

When everything is a priority nothing gets done to our satisfaction, and without realizing it, we are no longer on the path to the life we're striving to create. As hard as it is, we must allow ourselves to place more importance on certain things than others. By setting priorities, we make our lives easier to manage; when we take action, it is focused and forward moving.

Everything can't be equally important at the same time.

Setting priorities doesn't mean lesser-priority items are not important. It does mean that everything can't be equally important at the same time.

Realizing this, I was able to cut my list in half and put myself and my family at the top.

Exercise: *Identify Your Priorities*

Make a comprehensive list of all the action items you want to accomplish in the next week or month.

_____

_____

_____

_____

_____

_____

_____

_____

_____

_____

_____

_____

_____

_____

_____

_____

From your list, select the items your gut tells you take precedence. Briefly explain why each is a priority over others. Cut yourself some slack; everything isn't a priority today.

Priority	Why this is in the top five.
1.	
2.	
3.	
4.	
5.	

What are some creative ways you can help yourself focus on these top priorities?

_____

_____

_____

For those items that didn't make the cut, what can you delegate, delay, or cross off as unnecessary at this time?

_____

_____

Maximize Your Direction Moments

Where you are in your life right now is a culmination of your choices and experiences. No matter how you may be feeling about what's going on in your life, you didn't get where you are by mistake. If you love your military life, then keep doing what you are doing!

If you are feeling lost or frustrated with military life, then shake things up a bit to create a life you love. Close your eyes and think back over the past few months. Is there a moment that took your life and your emotions in a new direction?

Maybe you stopped tearing up when the national anthem began to play. Maybe you didn't catch your breath when your service member came down the stairs in dress uniform that busy morning. Perhaps it started when your spouse's orders changed at the last minute, and you still haven't recovered from the stress that descended upon your household.

A direction moment is a moment in time that changes the course of your life.

A direction moment is a moment in time that changes the course of your life. Direction moments can be catalysts to help you live in a more empowered way. When you recognize and use them to your advantage, direction moments become turning points with profound effects.

Each of us has the opportunity to choose what to do with our own direction moments.

Thinking back to our afternoon BBQ story, there was a direction moment that day that became an opportunity for me. In fact, it became a significant turning point for our entire family. That day, that situation, and that experience provided me with enough valuable information that I could apply and use to change my actions and improve my life.

In that pivotal moment, when I realized that the people we were surrounding ourselves with were actually preventing us from enjoying our day-to-day life, I knew I had to decide which way I would go. I could stay on my current path of blaming the military for anything that wasn't working in my life or take a new route where I could learn to embrace this life. The choice was mine. Thankfully, I chose to make the most of that direction moment and our time in the military.

I changed who I hung out with and began focusing on what was going right. I carved time in my schedule to get quiet. I maintained a no-drama zone. From cutting the yuck to refining my expectations, I used that direction moment to change my daily behavior.

What are your direction moments? Capitalize on these moments and use them to impact your life. Maximizing direction moments will help you find your way.

Exercise: *Discover and Use Your Direction Moments*

The following questions are designed to help you reflect on specific moments in your life and use them to make the most of your military life experience. Make copies so you can use these prompts anytime you are faced with a decision or situation that could potentially take you off track or in a new positive direction.

Describe one of your direction moments.

_____

_____

_____

_____

_____

What observations about your life can you make that are associated with this moment?

_____

_____

_____

_____

_____

How has this situation affected your experience as a military spouse?

_____

_____

_____

What can you learn from this experience? Is there a decision or action you can take that will allow you to live your life more fully?

_____

_____

_____

_____

_____

Embrace Military Life

You have no doubt heard sayings like "Prosper where you are planted" or "Military life is what you make of it." I've even been told to put on my big-girl panties. These comments are meant to inspire military spouses to buck up and make the most of the military life experience—the ol' make lemonade from lemons idea.

When I think about my future as a military spouse, it's exciting to recognize that I now have the tools, strategies, and ability to take action toward a happy and fulfilling life. I have the power to plan, prepare, and move forward. I no longer feel as if the military has more impact on my life than I do!

Still, taking action can be a little scary at times. I know my comfort zone, and diving in when I don't know the outcome is hard. It's like playing a game and having the rules change just before halftime.

Think about why you picked up this book and started reading it. Were you looking for a new lemonade recipe? What aspect of military life felt upside down? Which of the right side up tools and strategies resonates most for you? Does taking the next step feel a bit scary or overwhelming?

Taking action—the step that comes after you decide how you will respond to change—is the only way to move past fear of the unknown. It's what stops the second guesses and self-doubt and breaks through the obstacles and challenges that change brings.

Taking action is very much like using the old road atlas my father carried in his car. He would start out with his destination, pull out the map, circle his target, and follow the lines, knowing that if he did just what it said, he would get to where he wanted to go. Occasionally, he had to alter his route along the way. Sometimes he even had to change his plan entirely. But even he would admit that the journey is the best part. The journey is the best part of military life, too, and taking action is what sets that journey in motion.

The tools and strategies in this book can help you with the everyday challenges of military life—calming the chaos, flushing the stress, and responding to change. The personal challenges to take care of yourself first, cut the yuck, refine your expectations, and manage your reactions, can help you find joy and become stronger and more resilient.

While any of the skills in this book can improve your life, when used together they conjure a new kind of magic that offers a peace and happiness no change or challenge can take away—a magic that will help you feel great about yourself and be a better spouse, parent, friend, and battle buddy.

I challenge you to take action and make this book your own—go back through it and add notes that help you figure out your own situations and which strategies work best for you. Discover and use your own direction moments. Begin and end your day with a positive mind-set. You can do this!

Don't start using all the tools at once. Pick one or two, give them a try for a while, then come back and try one or two more at a later date. Update your notes.

Ultimately, the recipe you create will help you go way beyond the everyday challenges to truly *embrace* military life.

Exercise: *Bring It All Together*

What are your favorite ideas from this book?

_____

_____

_____

_____

How has your perspective changed? What areas of your life are better already?

_____

_____

_____

What else can you focus on to help you embrace military life today?

_____

_____

_____

Who can you share this book's strategies with so they can begin to thrive as a military spouse?

_____

_____

_____

Complete and Use Your Right Side Up Plan

Add your thoughts from this chapter to your personalized Right Side Up Plan.

Read over the notes and ideas you've added to your plan. Think about ways you can use your plan to respond in the moment when military life starts turning you upside down. Use your personalized plan to help you embrace this military life and live right side up!

In the Moment

Your Right Side Up Plan

The information and ideas in this book are only helpful if you use them in your own way in your own life! In the thick of the moment, when you are facing your own unique situations, what strategies might work for you? Which ideas seem to fit your personality and lifestyle?

Living right side up takes practice. Your personalized Right Side Up Plan is your cheat sheet. Write down your key takeaways from each section of the book. Add other ideas and strategies you think might work for you. Try them. Then come back and make more notes about what is or is not working for you.

Over time, the best strategies for you will become second nature. In the meantime, use the next several pages as your own road map to find your way when military life turns you upside down. I wish you all the best on your journey to living right side up and fully embracing military life!

One: Finding My Firm Footing

My Military Spouse Role

_____

_____

_____ » Ask a veteran spouse I
admire to be my mentor.
_____ » Talk with my spouse about
our expectations of military
spouses.

_____

_____

_____

_____

My Flexibility

_____

_____

_____

_____

_____

_____

» Remember: it's not a go until it goes.   _____
» Do something spontaneous. Skip cleaning
and surprise my spouse with a picnic lunch.   _____
» Change my routine for a day or two.   _____

My Support System

_____   » Find a battle buddy.
                                          » Get involved in social activities
_____   outside the military community.
                                          » Call a friend to chat.
_____   » Schedule a play date or lunch
                                          with someone in a similar situation.
_____

_____

_____

_____

_____

_____

My Healthy Mind-set

_____

_____

_____

» Replace negative
thoughts with positive ones.   _____
» Start my day with
meditation or prayer.   _____
» Stop the twirl.
» Focus on things that are   _____
going right in my life.
» Take a walk outside.   _____
» Learn a new skill.

My Resiliency

_____
» *Drink water.*
» *Take a power nap.*
_____
» *Learn new coping*
skills.

_____

_____

_____

_____

Two: Composing My Calm World

My Quiet Zone

_____

_____

_____

» *Turn down the volume.*
» *Step away from a situation and*
breathe deeply.
» *Spend five minutes doing yoga*
or stretching.

_____

_____

_____

_____

_____

_____

My No-Drama Zone

_____

_____

_____

_____

_____

_____

_____

_____

» Become a gossip repellent.
» If it's not nice, don't say it. THINK before I speak.
» Don't play the "my life is worse" game.

My Reactions

_____

_____

_____

_____

_____

» Interact with my life rather than react to it.
» Take a time out.
» Become a better listener.
» Avoid people and situations that trigger my tornado of intensity.

_____

_____

_____

_____

_____

My Boundaries

_____

_____

_____

_____

_____

» Say no.   _____
» Create healthy habits.
» Don't be a victim.   _____
» Don't procrastinate.
» Ask for help when I need it.   _____

My End of Day

_____

_____

_____

_____

_____

_____

» Spend the last five minutes of the day   _____
focusing on good things.
» Turn off all electronics thirty minutes   _____
before bed.
» Take a hot bath to relax.   _____

Three: Purging My Stress

Taking Care of Me

_____

_____

_____ » Schedule time for
                                    myself each day.
_____ » Listen to what my
                                    body, mind, and soul
_____ tell me they need.

_____

_____

My No-Yuck Menu

_____

_____

» Limit my use of food and   _____
chemical crutches.
» Let go of an activity before   _____
committing to another.
» No fear, no worry; only hopeful   _____
what ifs.
                                    _____

_____

_____

_____

_____

My Inspiration

_____

_____

_____

_____

» Find quotes, articles, cartoons   _____
that help me think positively.
» Be hopeful.   _____
» Excuse myself from negative
conversations.   _____
» Spend time with positive friends. _____

_____

My Motivating Movement

_____

_____

_____

_____

_____   » Find a walking buddy/
                                                accountability partner.
_____ ——————   » Take a fun exercise class.
                                                » Coach a sports team.
_____   » Stretch each morning.

_____

_____

My Faith

_____   » *Enjoy nature.*
                                           » *Join a Bible study or*
_____   *spiritual group.*
                                           » *Gain strength from faith.*
_____

_____

_____

_____

_____

_____

Four: Managing My Change in Plans

My Acceptance of Change

_____

_____

_____

» *Change is a process.*   _____
» *Set realistic expectations.*
» *I control my response.*   _____

_____

_____

_____

_____

_____

My Reset/Regroup Strategy

_____

_____   » Reflect on how I've
                                             grown through change.
_____   » Filter advice.
                                             » Hit the reset button.
_____

_____

_____

_____

_____

My On-the-Fly Approach

_____

_____

_____

_____

_____

» Let go of the things   _____
I have no control over.
» Gather facts.   _____
» Don't force a
solution or timeline.   _____
» Choose the best
option at the time.   _____

Five: Moving Forward My Way

My Priorities

_____
_____
_____
_____
_____
_____
_____
_____

» Focus on what's most important today.
» Delegate.
» Wait a day before saying yes.

My Direction Moments

_____
_____

» Recognize and use lessons from pivotal moments in my life.

_____
_____
_____
_____
_____
_____

My Action Plan

_____

_____   » Tap into resources
                                                and experience
_____   around me.
                                                » One step sets my
_____   journey in motion.

_____

_____

_____

_____

My Ideas for Embracing Military Life

_____

_____

_____

_____

_____

_____

_____

» Envision my ideal life.   _____
» Share the parts of military life that are
rewarding to me.   _____
» Mentor a new spouse.
» Go for an opportunity that wouldn't be   _____
possible if I weren't living this military life.
                                                 _____

Additional Notes

Notes from the book's exercises or my own experience or reflections that may help me in the moment:

_____

_____

_____

_____

_____

_____

_____

_____

_____

_____

_____

_____

_____

_____

_____

_____

_____